Missing The Links

A Mother's Murder of My 17-Month Old Son Garrison

The tragic murder of 17 month-old Garrison Burchett, and a father's optimistic attempt to understand what led to this tragedy, surviving this tragedy, and building a new life.

Gregory E. Burchett

authorHOUSE®

AuthorHouse™
1663 Liberty Drive
Bloomington, IN 47403
www.authorhouse.com
Phone: 1-800-839-8640

© 2013 Gregory E. Burchett. All rights reserved.

Edited by Joanie Gibbons-Anderson, Ph.D.
Illustrations by Robert Jew.
Cover Design by Lily Glass.

No part of this book may be reproduced, stored in a retrieval system, or transmitted by any means without the written permission of the author.

Published by AuthorHouse 9/5/2013

ISBN: 978-1-4918-1489-5 (sc)
ISBN: 978-1-4918-1488-8 (hc)
ISBN: 978-1-4918-1487-1 (e)

Library of Congress Control Number: 2013915783

Any people depicted in stock imagery provided by Thinkstock are models, and such images are being used for illustrative purposes only. Certain stock imagery © Thinkstock.

This book is printed on acid-free paper.

Because of the dynamic nature of the Internet, any web addresses or links contained in this book may have changed since publication and may no longer be valid.

The views expressed in this work are solely those of the author and do not necessarily reflect the views of the publisher, and the publisher hereby disclaims any responsibility for them.

Table of Contents

Preface ix
   Missing The Links A mother's murder of my 17-month old son Garrison. xi
   So here we are… xviii
   Acknowledgments xx
   Dedication xxi

Chapter 1: Growing Up and the Business of Life 1
   Chance Encounters 2
   My Gregory 6
   My Little Garrison 11
   The Troubles Began 12
   Lori's Themes: Anger, Control, Neuroticism, and Godly Conversations 13
   My Themes: Living in Fear, and my Optimism in the Center of Turmoil 14

Chapter 2: Centrifugal Force 17
   Signs, Signs, Everywhere the Signs 18
   The Eye of the Hurricane 19
   Missing Link #1: Anger's Extent 23
   The Viscous Snake 24
   The Phantom Shower Door 28
   Road Rage 30
   Missing Link #2: Sense of Control 32
   Mixed Messages 35
   Financial Oblivion 38
   Lori's Career 39
   Our Car 41
   Our Home 43
   Bankruptcy 46

Missing Link #3: Neuroticism 47
Separation Anxiety 48
Self-Diagnosis 50
Self-Treatment 53
Missing Link #4: Godly Conversations 55
"The Awakening" 56
Riding the Scroll into Infinity 60
The Telephone Pole 61
The Chain Revealed 62
Coping 63
The Inevitability of Centrifugal Force 64

Chapter 3: Evisceration and Emasculation 71
Days Prior to the Murder 72
My Last Morning with Garrison 76
Coming Home from Work 78
Finding Garrison 81
The Arrest 89

Chapter 4: Focus 99
My Focus – Being in Custody and the Investigation 102
The Shotgun 106
The Garden in the Garage 108
The Reunion 110
My Focus – A New Situational Reality 112
Reality Check #1 – Get Gregory Safe 113
Reality Check #2: I Need Help 116
Reality Check #3: Our Physical Health and Well Being 119
Reality Check #4: Trusting Others 120
Reality Check #5: Institutional Ambivalence 125
My Focus: Our Psychological Health and Well Being 132
My Strategy with Gregory 134
My Stepson 143
My Strategy with Myself 152

    My Focus: Being strong for my family, friends, and colleagues. 154
    The Woman in the Red Dress 156
    "Open House" 161
    Garrison's Memorial 164
    A Second Tragedy 169
    My Focus: Dealing with Lori's family and friends. 172
    My Focus: The Trial and the Public Arena. 175
    Investigations 179
    The Trial 180
    Attending Testimony 183
    My Focus: Confronting Garrison's Murderer 185
    Gregory's Visit 192
    My Focus: The Victim's Impact Statement 206

Chapter 5: Cranial Rectal Insertion 215
    The Chain Revealed 218
    Psychological Spin Control 219
    Self-Diagnosis Revisited 220
    Self-Treatment Revisited 223
    Planning for the Future 227
    God's Plan or Psychosis? 228
    Machination 233
    In Her Own Words 234

Chapter 6: Living versus Breathing 255

Epilogue 261

Preface

My life has been tragically shaken. My 17-month old son Garrison Burchett was murdered by his mother on February 23, 2009. A wonderful, beautiful young man who had so much happiness in life, and who was just beginning his journey, was taken from the world that fateful day. His life was taken in a very brutal fashion. It was ritualistic. It was grotesque. It made national news.

His mother Lori was convicted of first degree murder, in California's Riverside Superior court, on April 29, 2011. It was her birthday that day. She was sentenced to 25 years to life, and is currently in prison, and her case is was appealed. In California, all murder cases go automatically on appeal. When I first learned about her appeal, I mistakenly assumed that there was a chance that her conviction could be overturned, and she could be released. I found it interesting that her appeal process will scrutinize the court proceedings, whether Lori's constitutional rights were violated, or if there was any misconduct by the Judge, either counsel, or on the part of the jury. The "facts" of the trial will not be reviewed, at all.

If her conviction was overturned on appeal, it would all start from scratch, again.

It wouldn't end…

Her appeal was denied, on all counts. There are more options for her defense council, and I am sure that they are exploring their options. We will see…

Murders happen every day, some of which are reported in the media. Loss of life is tragic, but there are few tragedies which are harder to comprehend than a mother taking the life of her small child. A mother murdering her child is so rare, and so unheard of in the news media or in the entertainment industry like movies. It is so traumatic and so difficult to comprehend, that it is often not spoken of in a very public manner. It is hard to imagine something more counter-intuitive, something so dramatically un-natural, and so utterly incomprehensible.

A primary focus of Lori's defense strategy centered on a temporary psychotic episode, leading to temporary insanity, eventually led to Garrison's murder. This is a very short description, in my words, of the basic "idea" of her defense. There were other issues which were looked at, like anger management, drug use, and post-partum stress.

It is doubtful that you have ever met someone who knows of this kind of crime personally.

Missing The Links
A mother's murder of my 17-month old son Garrison.

This wasn't the original title of this book.

The original working title of this book was *I married a psycho killer, and I tried to make it work*. This was a very sarcastic statement, on my part, and was strictly meant as sarcasm. I originally considered this title to specifically grab the attention of a casual observer. I had hoped that a reader could look past the sarcasm, and discover the deeper meaning of *"and I tried to make it work."*

However, upon further contemplation, I decided to change the title, because I found that I had to *continuously explain* what it exactly *it* meant, and it became obvious that the working title should be more expressive of what my experience was, and still is.

I will never forget coming up with the working title. Following the death of Garrison, Mark Cooper, a very dear friend of mine, had been repeatedly trying to get me to come out of my shell, get outside, to do *something*. I always found excuses. Most (hear this Mark?) were legit. Some (hear this Greg?) were just because I was just depressed, and just plain not in the mood.

On the phone, he was teasing me about my continued canceling of our plans, and he accused me of being "afraid of commitment."

My initial, gut, instantaneous reaction was "what the hell are you talking about Mark? I married a psycho-killer, and I tried to make it work!"

Then the pause. The long pause. The silence. Then laughter.

What a sobering moment...

Missing The Links...

This title describes what I feel my experience was, in trying to examine why I lost the life of my child. This title begins to describe the multitude of factors which led to Garrison's murder, many of which I saw, many of which I was unaware of, and none of which I ever thought would have led me down this uncharted pathway. There were indications of trouble, there were "signs" of danger, and there were many "links" in my life's journey.

I missed those links.

This is a story of a father's contemplation of what he missed, of a fathers pain in this reflection, and in a father's humility by what he experienced.

This story, this journey, this tragedy, is extremely gut-wrenching. It is a tragedy of epic proportions. One that, on one hand, is completely avoidable. On another hand, our brains are a complex mixture of chemicals, and sometimes those chemicals are just messed up. The eternal struggle of "nature versus nurture," being played in front of me, like a theatrical production. Maybe, just maybe, there was *nothing* I could do.

I doubt that.

But damn it, I often feel that I let my child die, and I don't want that to ever happen to anyone. Ever...

Missing The Links...

I began this "project" as strictly a "vent-fest." It started as an electronic journal, a way to attack a keyboard with energetic vengeance, in order to put my thoughts and emotions onto paper. It was meant so that I wouldn't forget. I tried to include times, places, specific events, and my experiences. This was strictly from my very narrow, self-serving perspective. It was meant for my eyes only.

However, with time, this journal became immense, not just in size, but in scope.

I don't believe that I am a writer. I have always struggled with words, trying to express what my thoughts are. But, some stories should be told, no matter how difficult. Like baking cookies, you can't get to the "perfect" cookie, until you have made some really bad ones first. Of course, there are times where I prefer to eat the cookie dough raw, which would then nullify my entire point.

Life can't be learned, until you learn from it.

When I spoke to others (both professionally and personally) about what I was doing, often people would suggest that it may be of interest, or be of help, to someone else. At first, I didn't take their suggestions seriously.

But, in the time since Garrison's murder, I have had the opportunity to speak to groups, large and small, regarding women's mental health issues, about my experiences, and how there can be optimism, even in the center of turmoil. I have become acutely aware of how often women suffer from mental health issues triggered by their pregnancy. Perhaps this is due to the pregnancy itself (often referred to as pre- or post-partum psychosis), where seemingly "normal" women experience psychotic changes, often resulting in tragic endings. Perhaps this is due to some pre-existing psychotic state, having nothing to do with the pregnancy. Perhaps the stress involved with the pregnancy, Garrison's delivery, or the care of this beautiful infant was the final "straw."

I know of at least two distinct instances where my speaking engagements have directly helped someone. One was a father who finally realized that his wife was in trouble psychologically, and he stepped in legally to protect his child. Another was a young pregnant woman who realized she was having the same thoughts that Garrison's mother had, and she asked for help.

Hopefully my story has helped others, in ways that I am ignorant of, or in ways that I can't comprehend, and I never will.

Missing The Links...

This is when I began wondering if perhaps "they" were right. Perhaps my story could help someone else, somewhere; hence the journey from my beating up my laptop, to this book's conception, its development, and the eventual birth of this final product.

I have had many internal struggles with whether to move forward with this.

Perhaps Mark is right – I have an issue with commitment. This project has been an incredibly large commitment. Not in its writing. Writing this book has been extremely cathartic for me. I am speaking of whether I should have published it or not. The thought of people that I know actually reading it is daunting.

I now can imagine writing fictional stories. I can now imagine writing books on historical figures or events. I can now imagine writing textbooks to be used in collegiate science classrooms.

These would *now* be extremely easy for me to do. You can put forth an effort, and "throw" it out there for public consumption. Either it grabs interest of the reader, or not.

However, in the case of this story, I am exposing a raw nerve. I am laying out, for public consumption, my circumstances, my pain, my fears, my mistakes, my successes and failures for everyone to gaze into. For those who know me, this isn't easy for me to do.

I am very apprehensive about this entire experience. I am apprehensive about inviting you into my inner core.

What has given me the strength to do this comes from those few people who I have helped thus far. What gives me strength to write this book, are the people who this book may indeed help:

- The child who deserves the best chances possible for life, and the people in that child's life who need to step up and protect someone who is defenseless.

- The family, friends, and acquaintances of a woman whose psychological health is spiraling out of control, and hopefully help her to get the help that she doesn't realize or feel that she needs.

- The fathers, and other survivors, who are left behind when a tragedy like this occurs.

Missing The Links…

I think what makes this book so different, this story so different, and this message so very different than almost anything that is available, is that it is from *the father's perspective*. It is from the *husband's perspective*.

There are many excellent examples of books written on infanticide. There are many wonderful examples of books dealing with women's psychological issues, on post-partum stress, and on the rare cases where a woman hurts or kills her children. These stories usually are told from a clinical perspective, or from the mother's perspective.

But in my initial research prior to beginning this project, I have learned that there is *very little* in both the psychological literature, or in the public domain, that deal specifically with these topics from the perspective of the man involved.

That is where this story has value. That is where my message has value. From my seat in this movie theater, a person who is psychologically disturbed most often doesn't realize it. But it is the *people surrounding them* – family members, close friends, colleagues at work – who might actually see the warning signs. Most often, these warnings signs are not recognized, or are simply ignored, until it is too late.

Missing The Links…

How often have you heard "...he seemed like such a nice guy. I can't believe he was capable of doing that..."?

I hope that someone other than my mother would purchase and read this book. Of course, I hope that someone other than my mother would want to read my words, to hear what I am trying to say, and to *understand* my perspective and the *totality* of the story. I hope that this story resonates in a way that people would want to read it, to share it, and to talk about it. I hope that someone, somewhere, looks in the mirror and says "I am having these feelings. I need help." Or perhaps "my wife is acting like this... could there be a problem?"

Imagine being a family member, friend, or colleague, and really noticing drastic changes in someone. What a perfect perspective – from the outside.

I hope that the fruits of this labor and catharsis allow me to financially support the *Inland Empire Perinatal Mental Health Collaborative*, an organization that has become very close to my heart, and that has given me the opportunity to begin telling my story in a very public manner. This is an organization that was in the "planning" process for quite a while; ironically, I understand that Garrison's murder actually was the "final straw" and spurred them into action. This is a group of wonderful professionals who have dedicated their lives to helping women and families.

Perhaps the best way to help children is to help their families first. Offering a nurturing environment, offering counseling and support services.

Imagine a OB-GYN, or a registered nurse taking two minutes of their time to tell an expectant mother that sometimes women experience strange feelings of loneliness and despair, that sometimes women don't sleep very well after giving birth. Imagine telling an expectant mother that sometimes mothers feel detachment from their child.

Imagine a physician or nurse taking a few moments to say that they are just a phone call away. To look an expectant mother, their spouse or family members, or their friends and just simply say "call us for help if you have any of these feelings."

That is what the collaborative is trying to do. Such a simple thing. So many roadblocks institutionally and from a governmental perspective, for such a simple thing.

Perhaps this story can help in that cause.

So here we are...

I invite the reader to join me in this journey. Not to critically dissect each and every word, thought, observation, or description. Being critical is the easy thing that most people do. But *thoughtful contemplation* is more difficult. Think of this story in its entirety – always consider the *context* of what I am trying to say. I am writing this from my heart, but I am editing it through my mind. People who know me may read this from a completely different perspective of someone who hasn't ever met me. Someone who has experienced loss similar to mine would read this from a different perspective of someone who has never lost someone in this manner. Try not to judge me too harshly. Everyone is judgmental, no matter how hard we try not to be. In my opinion, being judgmental is quite acceptable. However, make sure that your judgments are based on facts, in the light of proper perspective. I have made many, many mistakes, and believe me, no one who will read this will be a more viscous critic of what is said – than me.

The cast of characters in this play are numerous. They range from my extended family, to my friends, to my colleagues, and of course to my close family. Undoubtedly, on occasion, I will leave detail out. Some of this omission is intentional, for which I have no apology. Some is totally by mistake, mistakes for which I sincerely apologize. These characters include the family I grew up with, the family which I helped to form through time, friends that became the family of my choosing, my colleagues, and my acquaintances.

In this book, it may also appear as if I am meandering and without focus. However, please be patient with me. There is a method to my "madness."

- "Growing up and the Business of Life" is meant to offer a perspective of who I am, and how I became a part of this tale.

- "Centrifugal Force" tries to show how a seemingly solidly normal life can be slowly ripped apart by introducing these missing links.

- "Evisceration and Emasculation" – my loss of Garrison, and the events surrounding his murder.

- "Focus" tries to explain how I dealt with the moments immediately following Garrison's murder, and how I have attempted to take life day by day.

- "CRI" – how my ignorance led to this disaster, how the pieces that I missed led to this disaster, and how I blame myself every day. Hence the title of this body of work.

- "Living versus Breathing" refers to my life since Garrison's death, and how I am attempting to build a new life for myself and my family.

Acknowledgments

Where do I begin? How can I possibly thank the people who have helped me in so many tremendous ways, how humbled I am, and how can I include every person who has meant so much to me? I fear that this list is incomplete, and for that I am so very sorry. So many have helped and my family. I would like to begin by thanking Sarah Smith, and everyone at AuthorHouse Publishing for their encouragement, support, and everlasting patience with me. This endeavor would never have come to fruition without you.

Listed below are but a few of the organizations and people (in alphabetical order) that I am eternally indebted:

Inland Empire Perinatal Mental Health Collaborative; RCC Nursing Program; Riverside County District Attorney's Office and Victim Services; RCC Early Childhood Studies Program; RCC Life Science Department; Riverside City Police Department; The Unforgettables Foundation. Marten & Teresa Anderson; Martha Arrelano; Carol Becker; Scott & Robin Blair; Susan Boling; Charlie & Julie Bow; Rick & Patti Brusca; Dawn Burchett; Gene Burchett; Craig & Cassie Burchett; Jeff & Susan Clark; Kym Conover; Mark & Adell Cooper; Debbie DiThomas; Lisa Dryan; Jaime & Alisha Fleming; Gil Flores; Preston Galusky; Joanie Gibbons-Anderson; Lily Glass; Gary & Cindy Greene; Ted Gregory; Monica Gutierrez; Judy Haugh; Tralain Hoffman; Chris Houghton; Eric & Rainey Hurst; Brad Irvin; Robert Jew; Steve & Michelle Jordahl; Carolyn Kegarice; Kevin & Timeree Kristell; Linda Lacy; Rebecca Loomis; Mike & May Lorah; Tom & Ann Loza; Diana MacDougal; Richard & Cindy Mahon; Diane Marsh; Dan Martinez; Tina MacArthur; Marilyn Martinez-Flores; Jon & Robin Matthews; Virginia McKee-Leone; Robert & Melinda Miles; Tom & Tashia Miner;

Mike & Hennie Monteleone; Sid Morel; Kathy Nabours; Nick Pate; Ken & Lisa Patterson; Dayna Peterson Mason Gregg; Bill Phelps; Brittany Randall; Chris & Susanne Rocco; John & Carol Rosario; Marj Rust; Terry Shaw; Heather Smith; Chikako Takeshita; Julie Taylor; Rana Tayyar; Michael & Tami Thom; Cassandra Thomas; Sylvia Thomas; Lisa Thompson-Eagle; Don Van Selus; Lynne Vazquez; Ron Vito; Peter Westbrook; Kristi Woods.

Dedication

This book is dedicated to my beautiful son Garrison, whom I miss tremendously every single day of my life. I miss his smile, I miss his laughter, and I miss how he played with his older brothers.

This book is dedicated to my beautiful son Gregory, who brings happiness and passion to my life each and every day.

This book is dedicated to everyone who may realize that something just isn't quite right, and who finds the tremendous courage to simply ask for help.

This book is dedicated to every child, who deserves every chance to live.

Exit Stage Left

Chapter 1:
Growing Up and the Business of Life

In this painting by Robert Jew as a gift to the author, the announcement of Garrison's birth is celebrated in a very special way.

It's interesting, the juxtaposition of personal humanity. At our core, we are social creatures, yet we strive for individuality. Wanting to be alone, yet needing to be surrounded by others. Whether living in a group and forming a family-unit, or being alone with no one to either depend on, or be dependent upon.

The eternal fairytale dream of finding that special someone, settling down and being a part of something larger than yourself. This is in competition with the innate desire to be independent and free-spirited, a stallion roaming free on the prairie, with no-one to answer to.

I am a social beast. I prefer being with others, as a general rule, with specific moments of absolute solitude, in order to re-charge my social "beastlike" battery. My fondest memories growing up were of being surrounded by family, tons of my childhood friends, at our home on football Sundays. Many pool parties, lots of food, drink, and tons of laughter. These were some of the best times of my life. I am one of the few people you can talk with who actually enjoyed growing up, being a part of high school, and being a teenager. This is what I want for my son, Gregory. I want him to enjoy his being a kid, for as long as possible. It's also what I had wanted for Garrison.

I didn't get married at a young age. Thought I was doing the right thing – finishing my education, finding that perfect job, paying off my bills, purchasing my first home, and after (what I thought) growing up just a bit, opening my eyes in order to find that special someone. I wanted to find that special someone to build a future with, that special someone to grow old with, and that special someone to fall in love with. The "right thing" was difficult though. I made many, many mistakes. Heartless women who chewed me up, and spit me out. Women who were, without a doubt, some of most sincere, honest, and sweet people who ever lived. My pushing them away, and in turn breaking their hearts. My craving strength in someone, and being rejected. My trying to "save someone" and feeling empty inside. My total lack of self-confidence, with no sense of self-worth, in any interpersonal romantic relationship.

Simple truth – I wasn't ready for a relationship, at all.

Chance Encounters

Garrison's mother Lori and I met by total accident. A fortuitous mixture of timing, and of circumstance. I am an Associate

Missing The Links

Professor of Biology at Riverside City College, and I had been selected by the administration to attend a conference on curriculum development in San Diego in 2003. I spent three days there, with colleagues from my school. I had a wonderful time. It was a very good learning experience, in one of the most beautiful cities in the world.

Lori was also at the conference. We never actually met, though.

It turns out she worked at Mt. San Jacinto Community College, within a 30-minute drive of where I lived and worked. It turns out that she knew most everyone I worked with. It turns out that during a group discussion, that my participation had grabbed her attention. She had realized that I was from Riverside, and she had been "checking me out" during those few days through my colleagues that she also knew. It turns out she had the "scoop" on me, long before I ever heard her voice. It turns out everyone told her how "wonderful" I was.

It turns out that my life changed that weekend, for both good, and bad.

Throughout the weekend meetings, we had exchanged glances, but hadn't met. At the concluding meeting, she walked up to me and handed me her business card.

"I think you want this."

I said thank you, and handed her my card.

That was it – no conversation, no getting to know one another, nothing else. Honestly, I didn't think anything more of it, and based on my personal history, I didn't think that anything would happen.

She did, though.

Two days later, she sent me an email. The next week, we met for dinner.

Some may think that she acted in a predatory fashion, and I was her "prey" in how we met. I don't think so, but perhaps I am mistaken.

She had a teenage son named Nicholas. One of my first distinct memories of getting to know Lori was being invited to his football practice, and us walking around the stadium and talking.

Life's simple moments, at their finest.

That was it. That is how my life changed: my responding to her interest, my being brave enough, confident enough, and strong enough to take a chance on continuing to do the right thing by sharing my life with who I believed at the time was that special someone.

Like the classic western – The Good, The Bad, and The Ugly.

That is life…

This is life…

The good moments, the bad times, and the incredibly ugly.

Looking back, it seems that our life, once we decided to join forces after two years of dating, was a whirlwind. Lori moved into my home at Riverside, and we had discussions on whether to renovate that house, or to find another home. We eventually purchased a home together, and it seemed life was good.

Missing The Links

I love to open my home to people. I love to cook for people. Whenever I have people come for a visit, I am like a busy bee all over the place, and that suits me just fine. Perhaps this is a reflection of my childhood, with crowds of friends over, and my mother being frantic (in a good way) providing for everyone. I love it.

This time of my life was also very hurtful for me. On one hand, I wanted to be inclusive and be surrounded by those who loved me. On the other hand, there was a growing division and rift between me and my family.

When my family met Lori initially, they liked her. But, as time passed, they grew to dislike many things that she said or did. I did not have their support in my relationship with Lori. I did not have family support for our wedding; I did not have family support during our pregnancy, and during Gregory's birth.

Lori and I had planned on getting married prior to our getting pregnant with Gregory. We had plans on when we would be getting married, and then our pregnancy changed the time frame, and affected our wedding plans. Because of my relationship with my family, we decided to elope for our marriage.

After thoughtful consideration, we invited two of my closest friends, and Lori and I got married, with just the four of us, in a very simple fashion. I am so thankful that my friends said they would go with us – I had invited lots of other people, and there were many gracious apologies, many reasonable excuses. But alas, they all answered no to my invitations. I love and respect each and every person I invited to be part of that day, and have no regrets for those who were unable or unwilling to make it. I also have no regrets to those I chose not to invite. I preferred to be surrounded by people who supported me, as opposed to those who pretended to. As it turns out the four of us, spending a wonderful weekend together, made my moment worth remembering.

Lori and I were now married, having just purchased our home together, and were about to give birth to Gregory. I was told on multiple occasions by multiple people that these are the three toughest things a person goes through in their life, and we were doing them all at once! We got married, we were pregnant, and we bought a new home! It was tough, but it was all good as well.

As I sit here writing this just now, and my remembering those conversations, how little did I know.

My Gregory

Gregory was born on August 28, 2005. I was alone at the hospital, alone in the waiting area, alone in the hallways. I was scared to death. No family, no friends – no one was there with me. To their credit, my parents and other members of my family would have probably been there had I asked. But to be honest, I feared more stress would be caused by their presence.

One week prior to Gregory being born, I had a dream. Lori was giving birth, and it was a difficult delivery. She died giving birth, and I was left with to raise a son. This was more than a dream – it was a very real nightmare.

When I had the dream, I woke up quite shaken. Lori had asked me what was wrong. I tried to deny anything was troubling me, but she was successful in getting me to admit my dream. My telling her about my "vision" was troubling (obviously) to her. She consistently has said that her dreams can predict the future, and if you spoke with her she would give you multiple "examples" of how this is true. In my experience, my dreams were never predictive, and I don't claim to be able to see into the future. However, her experiences led her to question her near "future" while giving birth to Gregory.

When I met Lori, she already had one young son, Nick, from her second husband. Lori also had another daughter, from her first marriage. I thought because she had two children previously, that she had lots of experience, and this "having a kid thing" should be a piece of cake, no problems, and all should be good. You try to tell this to yourself, and you hear others say it as well. But statistically speaking, any one of ten-thousand things could go wrong for you not to have a happy, healthy child. There is always reason for concern.

Most people say that statistics *suck*. Generally speaking they don't have a clue what statistics actually are, or how they should be used. Unfortunately, the reality of what statistics illustrates can suck. Big time.

Lori went into labor. We went into the hospital, and were told that we needed to induce labor. Gregory was under physical stress, and the physicians wanted to help him along. Lori did not want to induce labor. She had always had an easy time giving birth, and she didn't think there was a problem now. Against her wishes, Lori was given medicine to induce labor. Gregory's stress levels went through the roof. Lori was very upset, and she exploded on the nurses and doctors. She then made the decision to go home (against all of our wishes). I wanted her to calm down, so I took her home. I was nervous to begin with, dismayed at how Lori acted, and scared to death. Lori felt that it was the hospital's fault that the baby was showing signs of stress, and she wanted nothing to do with it. She hated the doctors, and she hated the nurses. I became the focus of her frustration and anger.

A very long day passed – then we went back to the hospital; Lori was still in labor. Nurses and doctors again advised Lori to induce labor. After some lengthy discussion, Lori allowed it, but this time, it got worse. Gregory's vital signs actually took a turn for the worse.

Emergency C-Section...

I can lecture to a large group of eager collegiate students until I am blue in the face about what happens from an anatomical, physiological, or surgical perspective, but until I actually emotionally went through this, I didn't have a clue.

I watched as they rushed Lori to the operating table. My knees got weak, and I almost collapsed to the floor. This was precisely the vision I had seen in my dream...

No one there with me. I made a phone call to my best friend Robert Jew. I don't remember much of that conversation. I remember pacing up and down the long lonely hallway in the hospital. I recall that he brought a sense of perspective and relief to me. I am fortunate that he was there for me that night.

But, alas, all went well. I got to hold Gregory in my arms. He was born happy and healthy, and Lori recovered quite well. It became apparent that Gregory's umbilical cord had been wrapped around his torso, as well as his neck multiple times – hence the physiological stress when Lori was in labor. It didn't matter whether she was induced into labor by physicians, or if labor had come by itself naturally. Gregory's stress would have been the same. Upon reflection, I don't think that Lori ever realized it, or if she had, she didn't admit it. Especially to the medical staff, whom she verbally accosted.

We came home from the hospital with a beautiful, living, healthy little person. I was so nervous. I was so scared. I was so proud.

The week prior to Gregory being born, I "threw" my back out. I think it was a result of the stress of his impending birth. But for about two weeks or so, I remember not being able to bend over to pick him up. I can laugh about that now, but I can tell you that it was quite embarrassing at the time. I also remember being happy that Lori had been a parent previously, and it seemed as if it would be "old hat" to her. In addition to taking care of Gregory, she took care of me as well. She kept me focused, taught me much about caring for an infant, and I was a happy dad.

Gregory was born just prior to the first week of my Fall semester at school. We decided that Lori should take six months off from work to be with Gregory as much as possible. What an exciting time! After Christmas, I then took some time off work in January, and we made the transition for her to go back to work. During this time, I stayed home with Gregory, and was a stay-at-home dad. I offered, and Lori gratefully accepted, to drive back and forth from home to her work daily. As Lori would often say, some quality "boobie-time" was a must. This served multiple purposes. Lori got to go back to work, and still got to spend some time with Gregory. I made the drive to her work at least once per day so she was able to breastfeed Gregory. This was well worth my time, effort and energy. Gregory's transition to a bottle didn't go well, and this made it much easier for Gregory. It was a lot of work on my part driving back and forth, but it was fun. Again, I was a happy dad.

I prepared to go back to teaching for the Spring semester, in February 2006. We enrolled Gregory into RCC's Early Childhood Studies (RCC ECS) program. What a beautiful, wonderful, caring, nurturing place. Gregory spent many a happy day there. It is a teaching program for students learning about the academics of early childhood studies, and it is also a day care facility, but with a twist. There are professional faculty and staff present at all times. There are teaching labs, where college students can observe, or participate when required by their classes. RCC's ECS wasn't cheap, but it was on campus where I worked. How lucky I was - I got to take him to school with me every day, got to go visit him between my classes, office hours, and meetings. I had lots of very good "eyes" watching him. I felt very safe with Gregory there.

This also allowed Lori to continue working without having to worry about caring for Gregory. It seemed, at least from my perspective, to go quite well for her.

From my perspective, as a proud daddy, I got to spend a lot of time with Gregory. I was a happy dad.

Did I mention that I love this place, and the people who are there? Little did I know how important this program would actually become to my life, and for Gregory's life as well. I will discuss much more on this important topic, later.

I was now a proud father, and I had begun my family. We got into our "rhythm" of life, between working, taking care of one another, and taking care of Gregory.

As much of life is, we continued our discussions of what we wanted out of life, and what our future plans were.

Lori wasn't very happy in her job – it wasn't intellectually stimulating. She had a Masters Degree in Education, and decided to complete a certificate pattern in ESL (English as a Second Language). This was part of our long-term plan for her professional life. We thought that if she could get a teaching position close to home, our lives could synchronize, we could take summers off to travel and vacation, and that our retirement age may have more security.

My Little Garrison

We got pregnant with Garrison, and we had decided that his addition would make our family complete. We weren't planning on having any more children, so during our hospital stay when Garrison was born, Lori had a tubal ligation. As we got closer to Garrison's due date, Lori still harbored anger and resentment over Gregory's birth, and wanted nothing to do with the same hospital again. A new OBG was suggested in Orange County (a little drive for us), and Lori was extremely happy and comfortable with her. When we arrived at the hospital for Garrison's planned birth, our room was overlooking the Pacific ocean. What an amazing place.

Garrison was born precisely two years and two days after Gregory (August 30, 2007). What an exciting time. It was a gentle pregnancy, and there were no complications. We had a c-section scheduled, and everything went as planned. I was not nearly as stressed with Garrison's birth. Heck, I didn't even throw out my back. By now, I was "old hat" in the parenting world.

In addition, I had more family and friends surrounding me. Although times were still tough (and strained) with many of my personal relationships, this time the birth of our second son was quite a bit more inclusive of others, and they got to share in my joy. I got to share in their joy as well.

Life seemed to be coming together for me. As is a constant them in my life, time, and patience, seemed to be my mantra.

Our initial plan was for Lori to stay at home for six months, and go back to work, just like with Gregory. Gregory was well-established at the RCC's ECS center, and we paid for and reserved a spot for Garrison as well. We had made plans, and were ready to go.

Life is supposed to be easier, when you make plans which are reasonable and easily attainable.

Garrison was amazing, and my seeing Gregory play with his little brother was one of the major highlights of my life. Even though he was only two years old at the time, Gregory was so gentle, and so attentive with his little brother, that Garrison really felt welcomed. His transition home was very smooth. He was a good eater, and sleeper.

Everything you could ever want in a growing family.

The Troubles Began

It was after Garrison was born that I think Lori started going downhill, in so many aspects of her life. I never have put much effort into trying to isolate when, or where, this "journey" began. However, as I have contemplated this (over and over) in my mind, it seems to me that once we came home with Garrison, Lori's way of thinking, and how she acted, seemed to change. Like snow melting on a mountain range, it begins slowly at first, gaining momentum, until it becomes a raging river.

Post-partum psychosis is something that I never had heard of. If I did ever hear of this kind of situation, it was referred to as the "baby blues" that a woman may experience.

I cannot, nor will I, blame Lori's actions strictly on post-partum psychosis. That is out of my realm of expertise, and that debate should be left alone to those who are far more educated than I regarding woman's mental health issues. But, I can't help but correlate these major changes to the time following Garrison's birth.

Much of what I will briefly address here will be covered in greater detail in Chapter 2, with the perspective of the "missing links" that I have come to regret not recognizing at the time. When I was living in "this" moment, these small details didn't seem to represent a major "red flag" as was illustrated after the fact.

Here are a few areas of concern of how Lori changed after Garrison was born. These basic "themes" will be used throughout this book, and it is my hope that how I present this makes some sense.

Lori's Themes: Anger, Control, Neuroticism, and Godly Conversations

These are the four "themes" in Lori's life, from my perspective. Her anger was a central part of the trial, and there were many examples of how she expressed this powerful aspect of her life. Lori was a very controlling person, and I think it is a fair statement to say that most people who knew her would agree with this. Her neurotic behaviors became more and more apparent though time, and became more obvious with her actions and behavior.

Sadly, one of the last areas of concern dealt with her spiritual journey, her conversations with God, and how this culminated with Garrison's murder.

My Themes: Living in Fear, and my Optimism in the Center of Turmoil

These are the "themes" I have identified in my part of this tale. Of course, these are from my perspective, but I do think they adequately describe where I am coming from. I didn't realize it at the time, but I do believe I was living in fear for quite a long time. Not "fear" in the sense that I was afraid of physical harm. Not "fear" of my children ever being hurt. My basic sense of fear centered on my knowing that Lori was quite capable of ripping my family apart, and I was fearful that I would lose everything. This fear led me to live my life "walking on egg shells" and constantly looking for red-flags that would cause Lori distress, and trying my best to "fix" those little problems. My methods of "coping" with Lori, coping with the situations that would come up, and coping with her daily were numerous. Many seemed to work, and many more didn't. But this "coping" with her was a daily struggle. In referring to "missing links" I think that this is where I didn't identify the problem areas which may have led to Garrison's murder. This is where I (rightly or wrongly) blame myself for what happened, and this is where I humbly want others to be able to identify, before the fact.

As you read the rest of this book, these basic "themes" will be referenced with more detail. As I began the process of writing down my thoughts, and trying to remember what happened (and when), I can't count the number of times I just sat in my chair, shaking my head, staring at my words in disbelief. How could I be so ignorant, and how could I allow so much to happen...

Looking above, it seems as if my life was a terrible disaster at that point. I must admit, however, that although times were tough, there always seemed to be a light at the end of "tunnel."

In the midst of all that was good, and there was plenty of good times and laughter, there was this sense of impending "doom" in my life. Not that I ever expected Lori to take Garrison's life, but I came to expect that she would leave me, and that my life would be destroyed in that fashion.

But, again, there was also a sense of optimism, and we constantly had talks about our future together, and what our long-term goals were, even though our short-term goals (and lives) seemed so problematic.

But try to imagine my swirl of reality - tremendous emotional distress, compounding intellectual confusion, and my feelings of helplessness. Contrasting, and amongst this, on the Friday prior to Garrison's death, Lori and I "celebrating" her finalizing the application packet to Riverside City College. We even opened a bottle of wine. She applied for a professorship position as an ESL (English as a Second Language) faculty. Although I don't know this as fact, chances are she would have gotten the position. She was more than qualified, having completed the certifications for teaching ESL, had more than met the minimum qualifications for the position, and along with her curriculum and administrative expertise, she would have been a fantastic hire.

Most of her angst, at least what she shared with me, dealt with either financial or environmental issues. We spent too much money; we needed to simplify our life; we needed to move away from Riverside. This was her mantra.

However, we had many discussions of what would happen if/ when she was hired again. For example, when she had quit her job at Mt. San Jacinto Community College (in hindsight I feel that this was a red-flag of her behavior) based on what she perceived to be a working condition she wouldn't stand. But, we were very optimistic that she would get this new position. We had many discussions on how it would be for us to work on the same campus, on how we probably shouldn't be on similar committees, etc.

We talked about getting caught up on bills, on traveling, and on raising our family after she got hired at RCC. There was so much to be excited about.

Talk, talk, talk. We were so optimistic.

I was so optimistic. I just knew, deep down inside, that if I kept working hard, if I kept my spirits up, that eventually everything would work out alright.

I knew when I came home, I would be greeted with at least two little smiling faces.

My optimism, in the center of her turmoil. There was so much she didn't share with me. There was so much I didn't know. I was driving on a foggy road that I couldn't see, to somewhere I didn't know existed.

Such a sense of oblivion...

Chapter 2:
Centrifugal Force

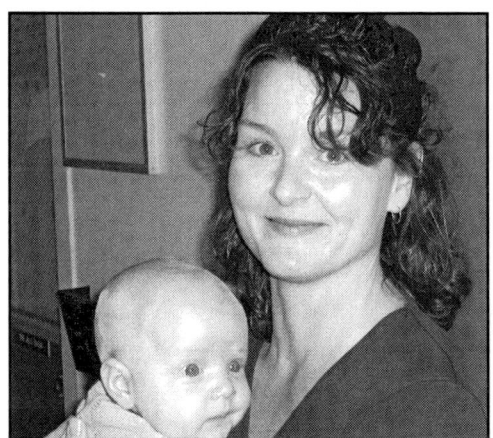

The contrasts of life are shown dramatically in these two photographs. On the left is a loving mother who is seemingly very happy. On the right is the booking photo following the arrest of a very troubled woman who just took the life of her 17-month old child. Booking photo on right courtesy of the Riverside County Sheriff's Department.

According to the Merriam-Webster dictionary, centrifugal force is "the apparent force that is felt by an object that is moving in a curved path that acts outwardly from the center of rotation." An analogy is the moon. It's traveling pretty fast, naturally wanting to "shoot" off into space. Earth's gravity holds it in orbit, continuously pulling it back towards the center of the Earth, against the "will" of the moon, and its centrifugal force. The never ending dance of two objects, consistently being drawn towards one another, yet always attempting to resist the spin, and the pull, away from one another.

When trying to describe what my life was like, this also seems like an appropriate analogy. My life was spinning out of control.

The faster it was spinning, the more "control" was lost. Imagine, the fabric of your life wanting to rip away, pieces of who you are, pieces of your life not in your control, flying into the abyss of the universe, never to be seen or heard of again. No matter how many pieces you grab for, there are too many pieces flying away.

Ah, the elegance of entropy, at its finest...

My grandfather Bob used to say "bang it to fit, paint it to match!" It seems like I kept my life together, my family together, my sanity together, by duct-tape, some glue, and good 'ole "elbow grease." However, you can't break the laws of physics, no matter how hard you try. As my world spun faster and faster, its centrifugal force became insurmountable, and now matter how hard I pulled and tugged, eventually I lost pieces of myself, and my life. I saw my wife spin off into space. I watched the fragments of my life fly away.

I saw Garrison's face fading into the distance, until I can't see him or hear his laughter anymore...

Unfortunately, it was only after Lori murdered Garrison that I realized the strength of this centrifugal force.

Signs, Signs, Everywhere the Signs

1970. I was just a young pup. The Five Man Electric Band. Not the Tesla version (although they showed respect). What a great song. How pathetic we are, when living in the moment, that we miss signs. Hindsight isn't always 20/20. It is human nature to become tainted by time, by our emotion, and by the intentional (or unintentional) distortion of the actual facts. However, my life and those missing links in my chain leading up to the murder of my precious son were like pieces of a puzzle. A giant puzzle, one in which I had no clue what the outcome would be. I couldn't even cheat and look at the photograph outside of the puzzle box. This giant puzzle, with an infinite number of pieces, each of which fit in more than one way with multiple other pieces, making perfect sense only after I and now you - complete it.

You can study every detail of a tree, and become an expert on that tree – but you still may have no idea of how intricate the relationships that the tree has as part of its community within its forest. However, these pieces prior to being placed into their moment, their meaning, and the entirety of their context, actually meant nothing.

Looking back, I did see signs. Many of which I would never have put into place. Unfortunately, there were a few which were extremely significant. I should have seen them. I should have understood. I should have done something. I should not have been utterly, ignorantly, blind.

Unfortunately. What a terribly unfortunate word, often used to minimize the severity of my ignorance. How unfortunate. How fucking unfortunate.

The Eye of the Hurricane

When looking for "signs," I have often reflected on specific events, and whether they have meaning. During my biology lectures, I often talk about the missing links that humble people in science quest to discover. Science consistently proves, time after time, that there isn't a single answer to any question, nor a single cause of any action. Often time people, in their everyday lives, want to find that "one" link to answer life's questions. This would make "it" so much easier to comprehend and understand. However, a "link" is one small part of a larger chain. An old football cliché "a chain is only as strong as its weakest link" is so true. Life doesn't have just one link. Nothing in science, nothing in nature, nothing in life, absolutely nothing anywhere, has a single "link" that easily explains the entire chain.

I have now spent years asking myself what were some of the "links" in my chain, which unfortunately led to Garrison's murder.

In the biological sciences, one of the primary arguments by those who argue against organic evolution is the "missing" links amongst the fossil record. Indeed, there are many lineages where gaps do exist in the fossil record. If you are looking for a link between "A" and "D," the argument would be that there is no "B" or "C." But, if "B" is discovered, then the argument remains "what about "C"?" Imagine the discovery of A, B, C, and D. Now the argument focuses on the "missing links" between A and B. How many links are there between "A" and "B"?

On, and on, and on, it goes...

Circular arguments. Don't you love them? No definitive answer, no matter how many questions are posed, and perhaps even answered. There will never be an end to this argument.

In the case of organic evolution, how much evidence would be needed to convince someone that the Earth's environment constantly changes through time, and along with it its living organisms? If someone has been taught that evolution is bogus, would any evidence ever change their mind?

In the case of a mother murdering her helpless child, how many links should have been discovered, in order to give a more "complete" picture prior to the murder. Is this at all possible?

Evidently not...

Of all things in life that seem so utterly incomprehensible, a mother killing her child would be high on that list. It's not hard to argue that.

Are people, who inherently live their lives based on an extremely limited and narrow perspective, actually capable of being humble enough to admit they were wrong, and truly change their minds?

How often does this happen? Imagine you are in the middle of a good old fashioned argument with someone you know. All of a sudden, the realization hits you smack upside the head that you are indeed factually wrong, and the person standing in front of you is, in fact, correct. Do you humbly apologize, or do you double-down? Do you dig your toes into the ground and argue with more passion? Do you continue the fight, just to "prove" you're right, even when you know you are wrong? What if the person you are arguing with gives up on continuing the argument – does that now make you right?

Unfortunately, many people believe that the "loudest" person in the argument is the winner.

A person's humility, a person's pride, and being factually correct, are often *the* losers in any emotional argument. Is there any aspect of my life prior to Garrison's murder that I should have identified? If I had seen these "links," and even known that they were a "link" in *the* chain, should I have done something, anything, to prevent his death? I am not even sure that I knew there was a chain, much less the existence of links.

If we are capable of identifying the links in a chain, eventually we should be able to understand the entire picture. If these links are known, then perhaps we can see a problem before it happens.

In predictability, you find beauty. In predictability, you find purpose. You can affect the outcome, if you know the signs before-hand.

So here I am, about to explain a few of the missing links of my life, which led to my beautiful son's murder.

My "eye of the hurricane" is my sitting in a seemingly peaceful place despite my deep sense of pending doom due to the constant turmoil, but unknowingly surrounded by violence. I had no idea of what my life was, what my future held, and no idea of what was causing this turmoil.

My chain consists of many individual links. And with any chain, it doesn't matter how strong they all are – it only takes one to be weak, and the chain is broken forever.

All of these, when looked at separately, may not seem significant. To some of you, they will scream out. I know that when I was "living the moment," most didn't seem to raise any major red flags. I, being eternally optimistic, would look at each of these as ultimately "insignificant," and firmly believed that everything would be ok. But, as with anything, time and perspective has convinced me that these were all part of the puzzle – my grand life's epic production, which led to Garrison's murder, at the hands of his mother.

Lori's Anger...

    Lori's Sense of Control...

        Lori's Neuroticism...

            Lori's Godly Conversations...

Missing The Links

These are the primary links in this chain. These represent the "missing links" from my perspective, primary examples of Lori's behavior. Of course, there are multiple links between these, which include my links in this chain, my living in fear, and my eternal optimism.

Perhaps other puzzles or chains can have a different ending – if the actors in those plays can see the signs.

Signs, signs, everywhere the signs...

Missing Link #1: Anger's Extent

What is anger? There is a clinical definition somewhere, chances are more than one, undoubtedly depending on the person defining it. However, in many cases, being angry isn't necessarily a bad thing. Focused anger has had led to many benefits throughout human history. Anything from winning a war, to being successful in a sporting contest, to finally standing up to a bully in order to gain respect – anger has its place. As animals, anger may be considered a vital part of our protective mechanisms.

But, living in societies, living in groups, or living in families, anger can rip apart the core foundation of security. Anger quite often overshadows rational thought. You may hear someone say "I didn't mean to do it" when they are angry. Abhorrent mob behavior is often the result of non-violent individuals caught up in a moment, where their anger and rage "seem" to take over.

It is said that most murders occur between family members, close friends, and lovers. Could this be due to momentary loss of control because of this anger?

Are any of us really in control, under all circumstances, at all times? That is a scary question, because of its potential answer.

We don't have all the answers. We would be fortunate to be intelligent enough just to ask good questions. However, anger seems to be a vital component of who we are, and we are locked in an eternal struggle to cope with, and control, our anger.

There were lots of examples of Lori's anger. Some of which were justified, some of which didn't make sense. Her anger management issues were a primary prosecutorial focus in her trial.

Here are three examples:

The Viscous Snake

Prior to Lori and I meeting, I had been given two snakes by the California Department of Fish and Game, as part of my experiences as a field biologist and an environmental consultant. They were taken illegally from nature, could not be returned into nature, and needed a good home. I didn't necessarily want snakes, but I agreed to take them. These were easy pets to take care of, with little effort. I wasn't too emotionally attached to my pet snakes, if you were so inclined to ask.

To say that Lori didn't like snakes would be an understatement.

Phobias are very interesting. Normally, people can be hesitant about something, until they actually learn about it. But for some people, the phobia and anxiety cannot be overcome. I know people who are scared of spiders, and will even react wildly when they see a *photograph* of a spider, even though they know

Missing The Links

there is no possible reason to be scared of a photograph. What an excellent example of emotions triumphing over intellect.

I had the snakes in two separate aquariums, in a spare bedroom that I was using as an office. Lori never knew I had the snakes in my home, until one day, during a conversation, I mentioned that I had these two little creatures. She wasn't happy. She told me that if I ever wanted her to visit my home again, I should get rid of them. Some readers may think that this was not an entirely unreasonable request. However, through some slick talking on my end, I convinced her that it was "impossible" for the snakes to get out. She seemed satisfied with my explanation, as long as they stayed in their cages, and safely secured in that room.

Needless to say...

I was at a meeting one day, and received a frantic phone call from Lori. She was in the kitchen, and there was a snake on the floor looking at her. She had jumped up on kitchen counter, frantic, yelling at me over the phone about this snake in the house. I'm thinking "oh shit, what have I done?" She asked me if it was possible for one of my snakes to get out. Of course, my instantaneous *save my ass at no matter the cost* defensive mechanisms kick in. "Of course not. There is no possible way one of MY snakes could get out!"

"Then a snake has come into the house from outside!"

Damn, chances are <u>that</u> didn't happen, and I was in serious trouble.

I kept saying to myself "Oh please, oh please, oh let there be a western diamondback rattlesnake that has come into my home!" I said this sarcastically to myself, but I knew it wasn't. It seemed that even though this would be a poisonous snake, at least it would have been *from nature* and not from my house.

I tried, in my mind, to convince myself of this...

I am chuckling as I write this, remembering how I felt. Having those thoughts and feelings of knowing that it was one of my snakes, but wishing it wasn't.

I quickly drove home. Pulling up the road towards my house, I looked in bewilderment. There it was – an Animal Control vehicle in my front driveway. I slowly (with my tail between my legs) walked up towards my door, and I saw the back of an animal control officer. He was standing in the doorway, trying to calm Lori, and saying in a very pleasing voice "Ma'am, this is just a gopher snake!"

Oh boy. He had *my* gopher snake in *his* hands...

It wasn't a snake from "nature." I lost any opportunity to put blame squarely on nature, and away from my "impossible" statements. Lori was truly scared, and she had placed her trust in my ability to keep the snakes caged. As with many people who are scared, she turned this fear into anger and rage, and lashed out at me. Needless to say, I got in some trouble that day, and I didn't have snakes too much longer after that.

Not that I could blame her...

This event happened somewhat early in our relationship, long before we got married, long before we got pregnant with Gregory. As I wrote this, and with some contemplation, it became quite clear that even at this early stage of our relationship, I was in fact already walking on egg shells . I now feel at that time that I was already hypersensitive to her moods, and her ways of reacting.

I dropped everything to come home that day. By the time I had gotten home, Lori had already "handled" the issue by calling animal control. Lori knew I was coming home, yet she decided to call animal control anyway.

We weren't married. In fact, we were seeing each other, yet she was a visitor in my home. It would seem that she should have respected my home, my belongings, and my wishes as well. I also should have respected her intense fear of snakes. Honestly, I didn't think the snake could get out.

Looking back, this example of Lori using an ultimatum to get her way worked on me. Perhaps this "set the tone" for our relationship.

I don't blame her for the rogue snake, for it was entirely my fault. But I now find it interesting how I reacted, and what my "gut" reaction was.

Perhaps my initial reactions were a result of the "ghosts of *overreactions* past" in Lori. Perhaps I already knew what she was like, and perhaps because of this experience, I was already "pre-programmed" how to act, or react. Perhaps it was the result of the "ghosts of *relationships* past" in my life.

Maybe this is just who I am...

Perhaps because, generally speaking, I always tried hard to please others in order to "gain" their love in the relationship. Perhaps because, generally speaking, I perceived myself as a failure in most relationships, and was very sensitive to hurting someone's feelings.

Maybe this is just who Lori was...

Perhaps because, generally speaking, Lori got her way, anyway.

The Phantom Shower Door

One day while I was at school Lori phones me. "Come home now! I cut myself, and I need to go to the emergency room!" Blunt, and to the point. I go home as fast as I can. There she is sitting in the shower, draped in a bath robe, amongst a ton of broken glass. Not glass actually, but that tempered glass used in shower doors and windows. She had somehow shattered the entire shower door. Now, this was not a small door; it was over six feet tall. She had this pile of glass chips all over the place. She had literally dozens of small cuts and abrasions from head to toe. There was blood on the shower walls, blood on its floor, and blood on many towels. It looked as if she were hit with shrapnel during an explosion. I collected her into the car, and I drove her to the emergency room.

My assumption was that, for some reason, she was pissed off. Obviously, in my mind, she took out her anger or frustration on the shower door. I thought she slammed the door shut, or open, for some reason only known to her. This opinion seemed reasonable to me, and still does.

However, she tried hard to convince me that it was an accident.

"I know you don't believe me, but I wasn't mad. The door was stuck, I pulled on it, and it just broke." That was her story, and she adamantly stuck to it.

I had no idea if that was the case. I never will. Lori was known to break things like dishes when she was mad. She also broke cabinet doors in the kitchen. Each time, I had fixed what was broken, if I could.

I can see myself trying to fix something that Lori broke. Being patient and meticulous, gluing, mounting, refinishing, refining.

It's almost like that is how I was trying to mend the situation, or mend my life. Trying to "fix" what made her angry. My trying to "fix" it, so that she would be happier again.

You hear of people being angry and breaking dishes. You see people throwing things on television. I hadn't been a witness to this before.

Was this supposed to be normal?

I know you don't believe me, but I wasn't mad. The door was stuck, I pulled on it, and it just broke.

I still don't know if what she said was true…

An interesting point - I contacted the manufacturers of the shower door regarding what happened. They assured me that this was impossible. Perhaps they were right. Or perhaps they were just "covering their ass" in a legal sense.

"I am just glad that you didn't really get hurt." I sincerely meant what I said.

It took me over an hour to clean up that bloodied shard-filled mess in the bathroom that evening. At least this time, it wasn't *my* fault.

Gregory E. Burchett

Road Rage

This example was actually a focal point during Lori's trial, as an illustration of her anger issues. Lori, Gregory, Garrison and I were camping here in southern California. While there, we loaded up our bikes to go for a little ride. I brought a little trailer for the kids to pull them behind my bike. This turned out to be one of my better memories, Gregory and Garrison sitting side by side, while I pulled them along. We then set off to go find a herd of cows along with their babies which were grazing along the highway that we were camping near. My boys loved to look at cows. As we rode slowly along the two-lane highway, a car drove extremely fast past us, and was quite reckless. We were never in any immediate danger, but it was startling nonetheless. As it passed us, it slid off the road trying to make a turn, in order to pull into the parking lot of a small corner market. I just assumed they were enthusiastically looking for more alcoholic beverages of their preference.

I was startled, and somewhat upset, but I thought it was all over with. I just kept riding my bike with my boys, just shaking my head, thinking about how idiotic people can be.

Then all of a sudden, I heard some noise off in the distance behind me, and I then turned my head around. There she was, my "tough" little wife, riding that bike as fast as she could pedal, chasing after the guys in the car. She was loudly yelling and screaming at them. Using very colorful language I might add, she officially informed them of their "ways." She was standing with her bike, next to their car, yelling at them through the driver-side door window. It was like she had *froth* dripping from her mouth, she was so angry.

Watching this, I had turned around, and began taking the boys back towards where they were. I was afraid that if they guys got out of the car, she would get into a fist fight with them. I thought I would have to get involved at some point, perhaps even to defend her physically. I don't remember them even responding much to her. They just looked at her. Perhaps they were scared of her.

I stared in disbelief as I rode towards her, and I experienced a certain amount of "shock and awe" as well. I definitely had a fighter for a wife, and on some level that made me proud, as her man. But then again, her over-reaction was quite obvious. When she "finished" with them, and began riding her bike back to me the boys, she said "Can you believe I just did that? Man they really pissed me off!"

Yes they did, and yes, you showed them.

Her reaction to this event seemed totally unreasonable to me, even at that time. At no time were we personally in danger, and I believe that she overreacted. But this is how she lived her life – the swings of her pendulum seemed to always be to the extreme, never resting in the middle, and she generally overreacted to situations.

I guess I was just learning how to go with the flow…

These three examples are but a small piece of this pie, but it seems like they illustrate three aspects of her anger. From something that wasn't her fault at all, to something that appeared to be an accident (and in retrospect may not have been), to something that showed what the depth of her rage was. There are more. There is also a lot to tell about how she tried to deal with, or even control, her anger. This will follow.

When she got angry at me, almost without exception, eventually, she would apologize. When this happened, she would tell me how much she loves me. She would tell me how important I was in her life. She would tell me she can't believe what she said or did.

She seemed to me to overreact quite a lot, and I got to where I could or would withstand almost anything she could throw at me, waiting for her to come back to reality, and realize that she made a mistake. I guess that this was my defense mechanism kicking in.

Lori's anger. My life spinning slowly out of control, and gaining speed and momentum. But I thought I had a firm grip on my life, and I mistakenly thought I was in control...

Missing Link #2: Sense of Control

Lori was very controlling. I remember her telling me that some of the biggest areas of conflict with her second husband after they were divorced were over the discipline and educational concerns with her son Nick. If it wasn't Lori's way, it was "wrong" and there would probably be a battle. On one hand, her opinions were generally right, when it came to how Nick should have been raised. On the other, it didn't matter too much if her opinion was right or wrong, it generally went her way.

I think that Lori was very fearful, and that her sense of control stemmed from this fear. I think that amongst Lori's largest fears were having to rely on anything, on anyone, or on having to answer to anything, or to anyone.

Perhaps her fear stemmed from her not being "in control."

Perhaps her fear of being out-of-control was a primary source of her anger. I have often wondered of how this relates back to her anger issues, and her unwillingness to compromise.

She had no control over that snake, or where it went. She had no control over those obnoxious drivers, yet tried to exercise control by being angry and confrontational with them. The shower door? Perhaps she felt trapped, and perhaps she vented this frustration upon it, causing it to be shattered.

There were many examples in her younger life, examples of how she could not trust anyone, including her parents. Her parents abandoned her. She did not have trust in her mother to provide a stable home environment.

Inevitably, Lori would either flee (just to get away), or fight tooth-and-nail to get what she wanted. Inevitably, she was always in control.

She joined the navy just go get away from her first husband, who as she said was a disgusting human, In doing so, she left her young daughter with this man that she had no respect for - just because she felt she had to get away. In this she exercised complete control, to a certain extent, at least in her mind.

She fought to keep her son away from his father (her second husband), because she wanted control. She was very much in control, or at least appeared to be, in most every aspect of her life.

This control stemmed from her not being able to trust anyone. This lack of trust in others began as a young girl being dumped off for months at a time with her grandparents, when her mother would go on a drunken binge. She couldn't trust her mother. She couldn't trust those who should have been there, and I don't think that she ever felt that she could find someone or something that was "safe," and where she could let her guard down.

I feel that Lori thought that she had me under her control. In many ways, she did. But I am also convinced that in many ways, she didn't. Perhaps it was this interplay of her controlling nature over me, and my sense of individuality, which led to many of our issues.

Perhaps deep down she knew she didn't completely control me. Perhaps I knew this even then and hence my fear of her taking my children away – something which she would have great control over.

Perhaps this is why I was so damned patient, and so willing to overlook many red flags in our relationship.

Or perhaps, my optimistic outlook is in my nature…

I am a lot like my father, and he was much like a pot of water. It took a lot of time, effort, and energy, to really get him mad. It takes a lot of time, effort, and heat energy to bring a large pot of water to boil. But once that is boiling, look out!

Some people would consider my being patient with Lori – and I do mean patient considering my pot never fully boiled – the equivalent of being a wimp. I believe that Lori thought this, as well. I don't believe that she respected me. I think she would have preferred my physically going to blows with her, in order to show her what her boundaries were. Our relationship wouldn't have survived that battle, and she would have indeed taken my sons from me in my life, but at least she would have respected me. Perhaps this is not the case, but I do believe that it is so.

However, I don't think she ever realized how strong I really was, and she never trusted in my strength.

In me, I thought she found that place of safety and happiness. In retrospect, I believe that I was just another pawn to be manipulated in her life; she felt that I was just another means to her ends. I doubt she ever respected or trusted me.

My fear of losing my sons became a larger reality in my life, and looking back, I don't think I ever came out and said that to Lori, or to anyone else. But, in hindsight, there were multiple threats, multiple ultimatums, and multiple circumstances, to which I basically swallowed my pride, and waited for "the storm" to pass.

I knew, ultimately, she was in control.

Unfortunately, if most men were completely honest with themselves, they would logically come to the same conclusion.

Mixed Messages

Lori began wanting to move out of southern California. The air is toxic. It has too many people. It is far too expensive. There were always lots of excuses, none of which made total sense to me, especially since I grew up here, and considering that my career was well established here. I always said that I would be willing to move, it there were a comparable position elsewhere. And I looked.

In reality Lori didn't care what I thought. She told me it would be "ok" for me to quit – pushing me hard to literally give up my tenured professorship, in order to work part-time at another school.

I guess this made sense to her, from her perspective.

However, this was unacceptable to me, and I am so fortunate that I didn't succumb to her wishes. I firmly believe that had I resigned my position, she would have moved us somewhere, and then divorced me and taken my boys anyway. I would have quit my job for her, and when she divorced me, not only would I be unemployed, but I wouldn't have my sons either. I feel that, in essence, she was trying to ruin my "total" life. I feel that this was the power she was trying to wield over me. Unfortunately, my opinion was later confirmed when I read what she had written on our computer in the months leading up to her murdering our son, Garrison. I discovered these after he had been murdered. I will share those writings later.

As an example of this emotional tug-of-war that we were engaged in, one day while I was working at school, she left me a long message on my voicemail. It was a phone message that ruined my day, causing a tremendous amount of stress. Let me paraphrase:

"I applied for a position up north today. I am going to get it. You are more than welcome to join us, if you wish. That is your choice. If not, I will be moving up north with the boys."

She hung up. I was frantic. I called her dozens times to find out what the hell was going on. She never answered the phone.

In the message she had actually given me the name of the college she applied to. I even went so far as to call the Vice President of Instruction at that school, and spoke to him. Upon briefly explaining the situation, he basically did an interview with me on the phone. He said he would love to hire me, but there wasn't a full-time position available right now. He would give me anything I wanted as an adjunct. He would give me project money to help their faculty develop their curriculum. He would make me feel welcome. But, there were no guarantees.

This wasn't acceptable to me.

I never did get in touch with her that day. While I was driving home, I was nervous and scared, not looking forward to my expected battle. I finally got home, walked through the door, and asked her what was going on.

"I changed my mind. Never mind. I am not moving."

She said this coldly, without even blinking an eye.

I stared in disbelief. My never ending emotional roller coaster continued.

I had to take a deep breath, and I walked outside. I was furious. As I sit here recollecting the events, I still get furious and need to take a deep breath. She really hurt me that day. Her level of callousness, her lack of respect, her willingness to let me "hang" all day – it was all so emotionally exhausting. I went from being convinced that she was going to take my family away, unless I quit my job, to her blowing me off, dismissing my emotional pain, and being so cold-hearted.

This was emotional terrorism…

This is how I lived my life in fear: fears of my unknown future, fears of my inevitable loss, and the realization that I was not in fact in control of my life.

I have heard many stories of how heartless people use children as weapons in a divorce. I could never understand how someone could do that.

I can understand that now.

Did you feel that big "tug" at my fabric? This one pulled hard from me, but I was able to bring it back into my chest. All is good – no pieces off into space. Yet.

I did notice that my life was spinning faster out of control, though…

Financial Oblivion

Everyone goes through money trouble. When Lori and I met, we both had stable jobs, both owned homes. I was completely debt-free, except for my home and one vehicle payment. I worked hard to get myself out of the "hole" of graduate school. After I was hired as a full-time associate professor, making a very good wage, I spent over two years renting a small apartment, paying off credit cards, student loans, and the cost of life. Then I was able to purchase my first home, a very humbling and exciting time in my life.

When Lori and I decided to get married, we discussed her moving into my home. Perhaps we could fix it up, renovate, and have some fun. Through time, I felt that Lori became less than enthusiastic about *her* moving into *my* home. If you asked Lori, my interpretation would probably be wrong. However, we did begin having discussions, at her behest, about selling both homes. We began looking to buy a place together. We found our dream home, built by two beautiful people with an eye for color and design that I can only dream about. We were both very excited: an amazing home, on an acre of land. Perfect. We purchased it, sold both of our homes, and even had about $200,000 in equity in the home. Everything seemed perfect.

Looking back, even then, this was Lori *controlling* what *we* were doing. It would have made more sense to keep my original home. We could have fixed it up. We could have made it "our" home. It was a beautiful home, in a wonderful neighborhood. It could have worked…

Like most people, many of our "issues" centered on finances. From my narrow perspective, this was to a large extent the main cause of our problems. However, from Lori's perspective, I believe that this was the tip of the iceberg.

Lori's Career

As I have previously mentioned, when Gregory came home, between Lori and I taking time off from work, we had about nine months total to be with our new child, and warmly welcome Gregory into our home. I always thought this is what planned parenthood was really all about.

It was our intent to follow this same time frame with Garrison, once he was born. Take about nine months off, transition back to work, and all would be well. It was during this time that she went back to work, and everything seemed ok. I drove Garrison back and forth to her work (more of that quality "boobie-time" as she referred to it).

But, one day I received some news which I didn't expect.

Lori had quit her job…

She bluntly informed me of this fact, as I walked in the door.

She had been back at work for just two weeks…

While she was taking time off, she would of course keep in touch with the people at her school, and keep up with what was happening, many of these colleagues were friends and acquaintances of hers. She would naturally get back to work, and seamlessly step back into her position, just like after Gregory was born. There were some administrative changes that had been taking place at her work, some of which she didn't like or appreciate.

She worked for a Vice President at her college. There were some aspects of this person's professionalism that she did not agree with, and there were some aspects of this person's personality that she had a hard time dealing with. But, as with many people in many work situations, you simply deal with it. I always thought she would be able to deal with it, as well. However, she went to work this particular day, and discovered that her boss, the Vice President, had unilaterally promoted his personal secretary, who had now become Lori's immediate supervisor.

This didn't agree with Lori. Not in the least.

She quit. There was no conversation with me, no consultation, no phone call. She just up and quit and told me about when I got home after work. She walked away from a well-paying job, simply because she got upset at her supervisor. We lost over $50,000 in annual income, instantly.

Lori was perfectly happy with what she had done. However, it did lead to a lot of other problems in our household, most notably financially. In one respect, I supported her, and I really wanted her to be happy. In another aspect, it was difficult, and it put tremendous financial strain on our lives.

At the time, we just dealt with it, but I do think that this was a signal indicating that she had more problems ahead. I will come back to this point later...

As I mentioned earlier, this was just a job to Lori, and she had plans on changing her career. She had really wanted to pursue a professorship in English as a Second Language.

Perhaps now would be a good time to go towards that goal with full intent.

Our plan didn't include her quitting though. This was an impulsive and unilateral decision on her part. This was Lori exercising her "control" no matter what the consequences.

The tugging of my life's increasing out of control spin began to gain momentum...

Our Car

We had a nice little VW bug that we purchased in 2005, but when Garrison was born, it wasn't practical anymore. We couldn't even put two car seats for our boys in the back seat of the car.

We had no choice but to purchase another car. We purchased a Subaru Forester, a car that I really liked. Lori and I argued pretty hard about this purchase – not *whether* to buy the car or not, but *how* to buy it.

In order to purchase the new Subaru, I wanted to trade in the VW. We had fantastic credit at this time, and it just seemed reasonable to do this. Lori was strongly opposed to this. In her opinion, if we turned in the VW, we would owe more money than we would get for the trade in, therefore having to roll the difference into the new loan. In essence we would have refinanced an additional $1800 for the difference in the new loan for the Subaru.

Lori objected to what she viewed as our $1800 loss. From my perspective, this made perfect sense, even though we would lose a bit of money. Our life situation had changed, and we didn't have much choice. We clearly needed a more practical car.

So we walked in, and purchased the Subaru, without trading in the VW. I had to now sell the VW privately, and just bite the bullet by continuing to make the payments until it sold. The biggest objection I had with selling the car privately, is that in order for me to pay off the VW, I would have to come up with the *cash* between the sale price of the car, and what I owed. This would have hurt.

After we got the Subaru, I tried offering the car to most people that I knew. If anything, I would rather lose some money helping someone that I knew. It wasn't long, however, until she decided that she didn't want *that* hassle of selling the car. She decided that she didn't want to continue to making payments. *That* was too much money.

She didn't want me to sell the car outright, but *she* also didn't want to make the payments either.

Tug of wars…

"Why in hell would you want to take on more debt? Call VW and have them pick it up. We already have what we need. Fuck them."

I was flabbergasted…

What ensued is one of the low points of my life. I wasn't behind on one payment on that nice car. We, (I say "we" but it was actually me) called VW, and voluntarily had them repossess the car. VW tried to work with me, offering me options on payments, on helping to sell the car, etc. But Lori wasn't interested in anything, but what she wanted.

I was exhausted, and I didn't fight hard enough.

They came and picked up the car. The car I wasn't in trouble with.

My God I was stupid. Our credit took a free-fall from 837 when I purchased the Subaru. I didn't have one speck against it, until that day.

Major tug and blurred vision from my increasing rate of spin. I was having to hold on tighter...

Our Home

Lori and I began having many conversations about eventually moving out of California. She really wanted to leave sooner (like *"right now!"*), rather than later (like in retirement). In her opinion, there is too much smog, too many people, excuse, after excuse. As time progressed, this became a bigger focus in her life.

Her opinion focused on not wanting our house anymore. She thought the mortgage was too much of a financial burden for our family. It was, especially since she quit her job. She had multiple "sound" arguments why home ownership was nothing but a fabricated "dream," realized only after World War II. She would argue for hours the value of renting, arguments against the tax "write off" of your home mortgage, and how saving money renting could be invested more wisely in other areas.

This is when Lori began pushing hard to get out of southern California, and to give everything up, and "start over." As I illustrated earlier, this is also when she was pushing for me to quit my job at RCC. Most of these "sound" arguments, at least "sound" from her perspective, were made about the same time.

I became more aware of a very humbling reality. As she had done in her previous marriages, she was very capable of taking my sons away from me, and moving away. My focus on this section is on her desire to lose our home. She ended up getting all of her wishes, in large part due to my just giving up.

I was exhausted. I quit fighting, I quit fighting for what I thought was right, and instead of fighting I tried to "steer" the conversations. I did this in order to try to keep my family together.

So here it is. As with the VW car, we walked away from our home. Our home, the one I considered our "dream" home. Our beautiful home, the one in which we had not missed a single payment.

Coincidently, at the same time, two close friends of ours had accepted jobs elsewhere, and had told us that they were planning on renting their home. As my luck would have it, this was during the same time frame that our discussions of moving were reaching a "height." This made "our" decision so much easier...

I remember sitting on the floor of our friends' home, when Lori asked them if we could rent their house. Sitting there, listening to her try to explain why we were going to walk away from our home, and why she was asking for their house was interesting.

Surrealistic in fact…

So we made the decision to move into our friends' home as renters. It needed some work though, so we agreed to replace the carpeting and paint it.

Lori took Gregory and Garrison on vacation. This was during the summer that we were moving into the rental house, prior to Garrison's death. She drove away with our new Subaru, taking my sons, on a trip that was supposed to last about a week or ten days. This would allow Lori and the boys to visit her family (which was important despite the history with her family), and to give me time to get all of the furniture moved, and the house ready. It seemed like "perfect" timing.

Everybody was happy…

So while Lori was gone with my family, I worked my ass off to get moved into a rental home. I left my beautiful home vacant, and walked away.

I hated that last drive…

Lori wasn't gone for ten days. She was gone for almost a month. She didn't talk to me very much while she was gone. Periodically, she would send me a photograph she had taken of the boys playing, in different beautiful places she had visited. She would leave messages. One in particular said that she didn't want to come back. She liked it in Colorado too much.

I called her often. She often wouldn't answer. This had become so common, in our communication.

Garrison learned how to walk while they were away...

I didn't get to see that. I remember a phone conversation where Lori was telling me about the boys. I told her I was done with the house, I missed them, and I wanted them to come home. It was time. To her credit, she began her drive home the next day. When they got home, I was so happy to see them, but I remember hoping like hell that she liked the house. I worked so hard. I was very proud of the new home that I had built for my family.

Just hoping that Lori would like it too...

That was a very tough summer.

Bankruptcy

Isn't bankruptcy great? We can spend all we want, give none of it back, and start from scratch, making our life easier and simpler.

This was the constant message Lori began to give me. Heck, she had done it once before, spent money like crazy prior to becoming bankrupt, and then said *adieu* to the debt.

Just like saying "fuck you" to VW...

I was very much against the thought of going bankrupt. We made good money, even though money was tight. We could live within our means. It was only going to get better. When Lori got a new job, then her income would be "gravy" and we would be just fine. I knew we were budgeted to live within our means, and if we were patient, everything would be fine.

In her mind, our home represented everything that, from a financial perspective, was completely wrong with our lives.

There are a few other examples like massive spending sprees of thousands of dollars on useless items, and her purchases of tremendous amounts of dietary supplements, which I will discuss later. After Garrison's death it became very evident to me that her intent was to declare bankruptcy from the beginning, and I was I was just a pawn in her life's drama.

I was a pawn, swimming in the swirl of my own reality, with her emotional state stirring the water in my pool. This is as good a description of how powerless I was, seemingly watching from a distance as my life was pulled apart by this unseen, powerful centrifugal force.

Missing Link #3: Neuroticism

Many of her behaviors seemed to me, at least in hindsight, to be very neurotic. Just to double-check, I did some research on neuroticism. *Webster's* defines neurosis as "a mental and emotional disorder that is less serious than a psychosis, is not characterized by disturbance of the use of language, and is accompanied by various bodily and mental disturbances."

Now that is a mouthful. Distress is a major component, and she did show distress. Another thing that I found quite interesting, is that delusional behavior generally isn't associated with neurotic behavior.

She had both…

Her neurotic behavior, from my perspective now, began after Garrison was born, and progressed. Eventually these "odd" or "quirky" behaviors led to more disturbing and troubling behaviors. In Lori, at least when Garrison was young, I never saw any evidence of delusional behavior. I think that this didn't start occurring until after Garrison was over a year old.

Separation Anxiety

When Garrison was born, we had a "plan" of what we wanted to do, and the time frame by which we wanted to do it.

As I have mentioned, Gregory was enrolled at RCC's ECS (Early Childhood Studies Program), and he was doing extremely well. I had the luxury of being able to visit him whenever I wanted, was able to take him to and from school with me, and he was being watched by dedicated and caring faculty and staff. It was a wonderful situation for me, and Gregory flourished.

We decided to enroll Garrison as well. It seemed so logical. Lori was going to stay home with Garrison, as she did with Gregory, for the first nine months of his life, then go back to work. We began paying close to $700 per month to reserve a space for Garrison in February of 2008. This was in addition to Gregory's monthly tuition, and was a substantial amount of money and investment.

Lori wouldn't let him go. It was during this time that she had impulsively quit her job after being back for only about two weeks following her maternity leave. Given the reality that she didn't have a job anymore, we made the decision for Lori to be a stay at home mom, re-focus her professional life goals, and move towards making them a reality. That was our goal, to get Garrison a bit older, and everything would work out.

That sounded so optimistic – sounds like me.

She said that she wanted him to attend the ECS center, because we both agreed that it would be a good experience for him, as it was with Gregory. Even though she wasn't working any more, we still thought this would be a good idea, at least for Garrison to go with his brother, part-time in the mornings. It would also give Lori a bit of time in the mornings to be alone, to do what she would like, and then when she was ready to pick him up, they could spend a tremendous amount of quality time together.

I also felt that when (if?) Lori got another job, presumably in the summer, that Garrison would be well-adjusted, and would be more able to spend more time there. Plus, I wanted to take him with Gregory – I found that this was good daddy time.

Lori tried to take him one morning. Just that once. She got very upset, and she went home. She was only there for one hour.

I never got the "straight" story of what happened from her. She tried to say that Garrison wasn't happy there, and so she decided it would be better to just take him home.

This was a completely different routine for her, in our lives. She never had to drop off Gregory and perhaps dropping off and picking up Garrison created a different emotional experience for her. However, because she was home with Garrison, she thought she could take him, now and then, for a short time.

I believe that had I taken Garrison to school (like we planned), and had I brought him home, she wouldn't have reacted in quite the same way.

We argued over this quite a lot. From my perspective, we would need Garrison there, because Lori would get a job eventually. At that time, the ECS was extremely hard to get into, with limited spaces. That is why I was so willing to pay for Garrison (we paid for 11 months), because I just knew deep inside that one day Lori would wake up, and then want to take him in.

Day, after day, after day, after day…

This was a prime example of how "patient" I was with Lori.

Stupid of me, huh?

I now think that Lori quit her job because of Garrison. I now think that Lori refused to let him out of her sight. I now think that she focused a tremendous amount of her attention and energies towards Garrison.

This, perhaps, eventually manifested itself into her attention to his "well-being" when she decided to take his life.

She said she did it, because she loved him.

Perhaps I have no idea what I am talking about…

Self-Diagnosis

There came a point, that Lori's behavior even got the attention of Lori. She started recognizing that many of the things she said, and many of the things that she did, weren't quite right. She often would say that it was the result of her stress, or money issues, or the fact she wasn't happy just being at home. Her living in California was also to blame. The food she ate was to blame.

At first, she said she was just angry. If she could control her anger, she would be able to manage anything.

Her attention to her anger issues then morphed, and began focusing on her mood swings. At times she would be angry, at times sad, and at times very happy. Unfortunately, I wasn't home often during the week, and there she sat, in this swirl of her emotion, by herself.

Sometimes being a stay-at-home mother can be prison, in and of itself.

As she contemplated her mood swings, she began to do research on the web, looking for answers.

She self-diagnosed herself as bi-polar.

She did this by doing *extensive* research on her computer. I think that this is one good example of her neurotic behavior – when she would "decide" she would want to know about something, she would spend many long hours going from website to website, thus becoming an "expert" on that topic. Her self-diagnosis, and her resulting decisions because of this "fact" exemplify what I am trying to describe.

I cannot say she wasn't bi-polar. In my humble opinion, she showed many of the classic signs and symptoms of being bi-polar. There are also clinical signs of bi-polar disorder that she did not exhibit. Definite times of mania, and definite times of major depression. I also think that her levels of anger perhaps came from a place of depression. Again, I am not an expert – I just lived the moments.

My problem isn't whether she was diagnosed as bi-polar. My issues with Lori were in the fact that *she* did *her own* diagnosis, and she was attempting to self-treat (discussed later) this serious condition.

Through our discussions, she did agree to talk to someone. At first, she spoke with our family physician. His initial reaction? She never told me. All that she said is that he referred her to a psychiatrist.

She did see a psychiatrist, and was prescribed some medications, at least on the short-term, during the initial stages of their meetings. There was no formal diagnosis, and I believe that this was because of the limited time Lori was under her care. On a few occasions, Lori was given some mild medications. For the life of me, I can't remember (or determine) what they were. She did begin these but didn't like the side-effects (either the actual side-effects she felt, or the *perceived* side effects that she "knew" would happen). She didn't want the medications.

Eventually she didn't like what the treatments were doing, and she didn't like what the psychiatrist was saying, so she wanted to see someone else.

She went to a clinic, where she was seen by a nurse practitioner. The nurse practitioner evidently wrote down that Lori was bipolar, and put her on some mild sedative as well. I understand that she testified to this, at the trial.

Lori didn't take those either.

The point I am trying to make here is that there was no official diagnosis of mental disorder. This was a big part of the trial. The defense position was that Lori was diagnosed, multiple times, with psychological disorders, and was seeking treatment. This would have bolstered her argument that she was criminally insane and thus not criminally liable for her actions.

The prosecution position is that neither the concerns of her family physician or nurse practitioner factually mattered, because neither were indeed qualified to diagnose Lori with a psychological disorder. The psychiatrist that Lori saw, who was qualified, didn't have adequate time, at that time, to make a formal diagnosis.

Of course, keep in mind that these are my words, and these are spoken from my perspective. I may be mistaken in some of the details or interpretations, and if I am, I will stand corrected in time.

Self-Treatment

There was one diagnosis that Lori received, and one that she wholeheartedly agreed with. She was diagnosed with anger issues, and the physician that made this diagnosis prescribed Lori with a medical marijuana card.

Once she got this card, this admittedly became her preferred method of self treatment.

I do know that Lori would wake up angry in the mornings, not even look at me, walk right past me, grab a joint, and in a few minutes she would noticeably be happier.

Is this proof that it worked? Perhaps.

If it did work, she must have been the angriest person in the world, based on how much she was smoking, and how much it was costing us.

Towards the time of her murdering Garrison, she was smoking over an ounce of marijuana every couple of days. This was causing an immense financial strain on our family, and an emotional strain on our relationship.

It got so bad, that *she* decided that *we* needed to grow marijuana, in order to save money.

Not that I could argue with her on that one – from the financial perspective.

Speaking of centrifugal force, and speaking of how my life was spinning out of control, now I find myself in the garage building a greenhouse to raise medical marijuana. In order just to save some money. I know I am a biologist, but really?

In addition to the marijuana that Lori used, she placed primary focus, energy, and a lot of money, into natural supplements. This was due to her self-diagnosis of how bad the food was that she was digesting, how bad the air was that she was breathing. She "discovered" that she was allergic to gluten all of a sudden. She really wasn't, but why would she listen to reason? Less than $1/10^{th}$ of 1% of people actually are (less than 1 in 130 or so people), and she had never experienced any distress with gluten prior.

At the same time that Lori began neurotically focusing on her diet, and she began embracing yoga, as well. After Garrison was born, Lori really wanted to live a healthy lifestyle (hence her wishes to move out of southern California). She also began dissecting every ingredient in all of the foods that we purchased. She spent hours searching for information (good and bad) on foods. She began to shop at a local healthy food store. I just don't mean shop; I mean she purchased a lot of food, drinks, and supplements. We spent a large amount of money there. One of her favorite drinks was something called kombucha, which is a fermented tea. This cost close to three dollars a bottle. She would consume eight to ten bottles a day at a cost of 24-30 dollars a day! Her shopping for these natural foods, and her consumption of products like kombucha, were adding tremendously to our financial woes.

I should have been the "customer of the year" at this specific shop here in Riverside that we frequented. I think I deserved it. I paid for it...

I will revisit these areas of concern, her spending money and the focus on yoga later. But suffice it to say, these (in retrospect) are examples of how my life was spinning out of control.

Missing Link #4: Godly Conversations

Here is a philosophical dilemma that, for some, is quite uncomfortable. From a legal perspective, it also poses many very interesting quandaries. I became aware of this during Lori's murder trial.

Why is it perfectly acceptable, and considered perfectly sane, to believe in God, and to speak to Him?

In contrast, why is it a clinical aspect (or sign) of medical insanity, when God speaks to you?

It's "rational" to believe in God, but can be deemed "insane" to actually hear His voice.

This is an important aspect of what is factually considered delusional.

This is a very interesting intellectual quandary.

God spoke with and to Lori, or at least she thought so. He spoke to her through music. She could hear His voice coming from the car stereo. She also felt that God spoke to her through visual messages and images. Lori said that God told her to do things, and go places.

Evidently God told Lori to send Garrison to heaven.

At least she thought so.

"The Awakening"

Lori got interested in yoga classes, and eventually even I started going. When we began, it was a chance for both of us to get away from the kids, to have some planned alone time, and to exercise. When looking at the calendar, the days that yoga classes were planned were just a normal part of our day. Lori originally made this suggestion that we go, and I agreed, because it seemed like it would be fun, and be something different.

What began as planned "alone time" a few times a week, and a good way to get some exercise in, at some point for her became something very different.

From my perspective, I loved it. I loved the physical aspect of yoga, and I loved inflating the "Type B" personality in my life. Learning to breathe, exploring the value of forced relaxation, and approaching every yoga position as a way to strengthen my back, were my primary motivating forces. I enjoyed getting away a bit, and even got to know the good people who run the yoga studio, and some of the other clientele. There were weeks when I would be able to attend multiple yoga classes. There were times when I couldn't make it, and it was ok with me.

Lori initially started yoga for the same basic reasons I did. Her focus changed quite a bit, though. She embraced many aspects of yoga, and yoga became a very important part of her life. Very much so, and as with most things in Lori's life, perhaps she took it to the extreme.

When she would miss a yoga class, for whatever reason, she would get very upset. There were times I would get home late from school, causing her to miss a class, and that wouldn't go well. She would yell and scream. I remember once going on a field trip with my class, coming home during rush hour, and her yelling at me on the phone about her missing a class.

Careful scheduling of her yoga classes became a vital part of her weekly planning, and I had to abide by that scheduling.

She began embracing the philosophical and spiritual aspects of yoga, to a large extent. I believe that yoga helped Lori open a door for self-examination, to ponder many ethical and philosophical questions of her life. These doors were like a dam holding a vast amount of water – when the door was opened, a lot of energy could be released.

I have spent a few paragraphs trying to give context to what Lori called her "awakening." I believe that this experience changed the course of Lori's life, and my life, forever.

What Lori referred to as her "awakening" was an incredibly emotional moment during a yoga class, and when she came home, she shared with me what she had experienced. In hindsight, this may have been a defining moment in her life. I don't remember the precise detail of what she said, or what she felt, but I do remember the enthusiasm of her experience. When she was telling me about it, she was pretty excited and emotional, and much of what she said quite frankly didn't make sense to me. That conversation is a blur in my memory. However, I discovered a tremendous amount of references of this day in her notes, and her writings on a computer, which I will share later.

During this yoga class, she listened intently to what the yoga instructor was talking about. She was so moved, that she began to cry. She told me that she excused herself, and went to the restroom, where she allowed herself to cry. Lori said it was a very emotionally lifting moment. When she had a moment alone with her yoga class instructor, she gave her a hug, and told her that she loved her.

It was after this "awakening" that her thoughts really became strange. Our conversations began to take paths all over the place. She wanted me to quit my job, and for the family to move with her to India for a year.

Our family took a drive to a beautiful small mountain town/resort one day. We played in the snow, and we enjoyed hot chocolate. We spent part of the day walking around, and looking at all of the small shops. One shop was owned by wonderful couple from Nepal, who shared with us stories of their recent adventures. They had begun a small ecotourism company, and had recently returned from a trip where they took six Americans to Nepal, Tibet, and Northern India. Their stories were wonderful, and their stories made us envious about traveling the world.

Lori never forgot that visit. I remember distinctly during one of our major conversations, when she was pushing me to move our family to India. She said I needed to take a year off from teaching, and move with her to India. To be honest, it was within the realm of possibility (I could have worked out the logistics professionally), and it did hold a certain measure of intrigue. It would have been a fantastic life-experience, and perhaps it would have helped Lori find inner-peace.

However, she progressed to push this idea with more intensity, and I began to resist her forceful suggestions. Finally, I suggested she go by herself, and that I stay home and take care of the boys. I told her to take as much time as she needed, and I told her that I thought she needed to do this, alone. I told her that I supported her, and that I loved her. I told her she needed to find her way and be happy. I told her that she needed to find her path to happiness, and if this meant that she had to move to India, she should do it.

I knew that if she did this, it probably would be the end of us.

I think she knew this, as well. She said if she did this, she wouldn't come back the same person, and that I may not like her. She told me it might be the end of us.

I said I know this…

That was a very interesting conversation. Sitting here recalling the moment, I remember my being very much at peace when I was suggesting that she go. I was very firm that my sons and I would not go, and that I would take good care of them, and that we would be fine. But I now think that I felt most comfortable with the *idea* of her leaving, and this was the first time she talked about going away, and not fighting so hard to take the boys.

I think at that time I wished that she had gone…

I did want her to be at peace, and I did want her to be happy. That is why I supported her considering moving to India.

But I found that I also wanted peace, and I passionately wanted my children.

That is why I supported her considering moving to India…

She didn't go to India.

I often wonder what would have happened, if I had contributed to this centrifugal force, and pushed her away.

Off into the distance...

Riding the Scroll into Infinity

After her "awakening," I came home one evening to perhaps the most bizarre conversation I have ever had. It was on the Thursday before Garrison died, I came home from work with Gregory, and as I walked into the kitchen, Lori was bouncing off the walls. She was so excited. I couldn't imagine something so strange, and as I remember what happened, there is so much that I don't recall. This conversation I am speaking of took over an hour, and yet seemed like a split-second, and an eternity, all at the same time.

We had purchased a small easel so that our boys could do art work. You could put a roll of paper on the backside, and pull new paper over the top whenever you needed blank paper to draw on.

Lori had taken that roll of paper, and ripped off a piece that was perhaps eight feet long, and three feet wide. On this piece of paper, she wrote a lot of her thoughts.

She said she discovered the secrets of the universe.

Imagine "doodling" on paper, but on a very large piece of paper, eight feet long and three feet wide. A lot of scribbled drawings. Lots of thoughts written down, many of which were connected by lines and arrows. Mindless little drawings. Extremely mindful drawings. Just like in those movies where a psychotic killer has written all over the walls, and is discovered only when it is too late.

One figure that she had drawn was all over the place, having been drawn multiple times. It was the "infinity" symbol.

Her energy level was off any scale you could imagine. She talked about God, the universe, and this infinity symbol. She used the ends of the infinity symbol as the ends of a spectrum. Any spectrum. She used anger as a spectrum. She used "ego" as a spectrum. She used homosexuality as a spectrum. She used gender as a spectrum.

I stared, dumbfounded, in disbelief. Here was my wife, standing in the kitchen, surrounded by food, dishware, papers strewn all over, holding my young son in her arm, as Gregory played on the floor.

What a vision…

I tried to ask questions. I tried to understand, but I did have a very difficult time with this. At the end of the conversation, she got so angry and frustrated with me, that she grabbed the "scroll" in her arms, pulling it to her breast. She yelled at me that since I couldn't understand what she was saying, that she would never talk to me about this again. She wanted nothing to do with me.

As I watched Lori try to explain this "scroll" to me, I felt my life spinning out of control.

This "scroll" became a central part of Lori's trial.

The Telephone Pole

Two days prior to the murder, Lori came home from the grocery store with Garrison. She had a strange look on her face. She said that God had told her to drive her car into a telephone pole, and *if* she believed in Him enough, He would protect her. My head was foggy, not sure what to think. I actually thought it was a joke. I felt a mixture of being scared, very angry, and wanting to laugh at her. I slowly walked outside and looked at the car. Based on the physical evidence, she didn't drive her car into a telephone pole. She appeared to have driven her car alongside a curb, either bumping into it or driving upon it, resulting in damage to the front passenger wheel.

Unless of course, she did drive into a telephone pole, and God in fact did protect her, just as He said He would. The car, therefore, was minimally damaged – just like she said, because of her belief in God, and in following His wishes.

How can I possibly argue with the logic of God's will?

The Chain Revealed

These four "links" of the chain which I have identified (her anger, her sense of control, her neurotic behavior, and her Godly conversations) are all indicative of a bigger picture. Of course, these links were linked together by how I reacted to each link, how I tried to calm the waters, how I used my "coping" mechanisms to deal with my everyday life…

But, as the title of this chapter illustrates, centrifugal force is something that generally wins.

I will come back to each of these "links" later, and try to put them into perspective. But as I look back at the entirety of my life's chain, the links now make so much more sense.

Coping

How would I cope? I would want my space, and let her be alone. Often, I would go back to my office at work, even in the middle of the night. I would clean up my garage, or do yard work. I would do anything to keep busy. I would try to work out my frustration, without getting into further arguments with her. I had discovered that arguing with her, even if I were factually correct, would invariably lead to disaster. I feared many arguments with her, because it was a "no-win" situation from the beginning. I coped by avoiding those particular conversations.

How often have you heard your grandfather or uncle say something like "there she goes again!" referring to their wives. Same thing for women dealing with their men…

Isn't this the never-ending struggle between men and women? Isn't this normal?

Perhaps I am a wimp. Perhaps I was a "yo-yo" in her hands. Perhaps I was actually being manipulated. Perhaps I was loving, overly patient, and in hindsight very stupid. Me, the eternal optimist, hoping everything would work out. Feeling deep inside that if I showed her unwavering love, support, and commitment, that she would finally realize it, and that I would come to her rescue (of sorts). I felt I was her best friend, even if she didn't know it.

She didn't feel that way – evidently.

However, the stories of Lori's wrath stretch far and wide. So many stories, ranging from how she overreacted on the phone to friends and family, to her rationale in quitting a perfectly good job at Mt. San Jacinto, to yelling at her nurses or doctors prior to Gregory's birth.

Perhaps a cold beer, a brisk evening, and a roaring campfire would give me a chance to tell more stories. It would also give others a chance to share their stories with me. Don't you just love being a life-long student? In life, there is always more to learn.

Sitting in solitude, on a cool evening or morning, next to a campfire is arguably the best form of therapy.

That campfire sounds like a good idea.

I have often been asked *"did coping work?"* I simply don't know. I think that my coping mechanisms looked for the "path of least resistance" and tried to work with smaller issues or problems, as they arose. I may have been successful in putting out smaller fires now and then, and I may have been successful in preventing myself from going into battle with Lori, but in the long run perhaps my patience with her was of detriment. Perhaps if I had gone "toe to toe" with her more often, perhaps if I wasn't so obliging in her whims and fancies, perhaps something would have been different.

This was my reality – coping with my fears, and trying to keep my life in focus and together. How can I remain optimistic? How can I continue this struggle, between my vision of a "happy" life, and the fear of what my life experience in indeed was.

This wasn't easy. Perhaps the prism of my eternal optimism skewed my reality, and perhaps this skewed reality on my part kept me from seeing the truth.

The Inevitability of Centrifugal Force

The never-ending struggle of trying to hold onto a seemingly happy life, of trying to continue to be optimistic for life, of living in fear that my life can be torn apart, with the inevitability strong forces which we are constantly tearing my sense of reality apart. Lori was spinning out of control. I saw some of this, I knew something was wrong, but I didn't realize the depth of her despair, her helplessness, and her sanity slipping through her fingertips like water.

Centrifugal force tugging away at my existence, my sense of being, and my life. This centrifugal force, so strong, often unseen, unforgiving, and unwavering. Centrifugal force wins. Things may just float away, off into space, off into nothingness, off into eternity, and off into oblivion.

George Howard Darwin, son of Charles Darwin, pondered many of these questions, and is given credit for the first formal calculations of the moon's rotations around the earth, and in forming the idea of "tidal evolution." Research has shown that the moon is moving 3.8 centimeters per year farther from earth.

Imagine that…

But if you stare at the moon every night, throughout your lifetime, would you notice a difference? If a thousand lifetimes stare at the moon at night, would they notice a difference?

If you stare into the eyes of someone you love, would you, could you, notice the difference? If you do notice it, could you wrap your head around the fact that the person you love is slipping away? The "image" of insanity that many have in their minds is someone acts so totally "un-normal" and strange, perhaps drool running down their face, and speaking to themselves in a way that would cause most people to take a wide birth around them while walking on the street. This "kind" of insanity would be easy for many people to see, even from a distance.

What about when someone you love and care for slowly slips into this oblivion? Perhaps we would never know the moon was slipping away, until it "shot" off into space. Eventually its centrifugal force would win. If this were to happen, how would we feel about all of those "moments" that we missed with our moon in our lives.

How do I feel about all of those moments that I missed? How should I feel?

How do you think I feel?

At the beginning of this chapter, I introduced the idea of centrifugal force. I feel that this is a good description of how I viewed my life. As the "swirl" of the moment engulfed me, as I felt less and less "in control" of my life, it seemed like the speed in which I was spinning was getting faster and faster. At a slow deliberate spin, I felt as if I had a lot of control over everything in my life. As my life started spinning faster, I still felt as if I had a great sense of control, and that everything would be ok eventually. My grip was strong, and I felt as if I could take on anything. But, as the spinning got faster and faster, it took more and more force to keep this control. Eventually, all of my strength couldn't keep up, and small pieces started to fly away. Not many at first, but I could imagine seeing them fly off, one at a time.

Like the millions upon millions of rivets which hold a jet airliner together, losing one here and there isn't such a big deal. Some are lost on every flight, but they are easily replaced, and the plane isn't weaker because of it. But if you sit there and observe someone taking one rivet out at a time, how long do you wait until you get off of that plane? How many rivets can the plane lose before it will fall from the sky? How do you identify the "last" rivet that keeps that plane safely in the air?

My life's centrifugal force began with small tugs, my life slowly spinning out of control, gradually spinning faster and faster, and eventually culminated in Garrison's death. Again, like links in a chain, the entirety of this stress on my life, the cumulative effect that each small piece of this chain had varying levels of intensity. I think this is why when I was living my life, and with the perspective of those moments, so many things were so easily overlooked.

My original working title of this body of work "*I married a psycho killer, and I tried to make it work*" expresses that precise point. I didn't know she was capable of murder. I knew she was troubled, and I did try to make it work.

I didn't know what she was really capable of, but this swirl was my reality.

Optimistically speaking, what else can do you do?

The first links began with Lori's stubbornness. Those links were joined by her anger, her fears, and her independence. Those links were joined by her thought process going from not being a very religious person, to being extremely religious, in relatively short time. There was so much "glue" surrounding all of these links that I am so unaware of...

After Garrison's death, and while I was slowly going through our belongings, I came across a yellow book. The book was based on a poem entitled *The Dark Night of the Soul* written by St. John of the Cross. It was given to Lori by *someone* at the Yoga studio that we attended. I vaguely remember her showing it to me, but at that time it seemed insignificant.

I must admit that when Lori first showed me this book, I didn't think much of it. I must also admit that it didn't bother me at that time that someone had given it to her to read.

However, about six months after Garrison died, I again found the book. I remember the evening precisely. Gregory was taking a bath, and I was lying on the floor beside him, in the bathroom. It was warm and steamy sitting there quietly with him.

The more I read, the more my stomach turned.

I tried to convince myself that I could finish it, but I couldn't.

From what I understand, the story revolves around the journey your soul takes, as it separates itself from your physical body, and ascends into heaven. It is about the pain associated with leaving your physical form, as part of your spiritual journey.

This caused my stomach to turn, because I realized that it was an important part of Lori's perspective during our most "interesting" conversations.

These are just examples. Eventually my strength was no match for this centrifugal force of spin. Sadly, I eventually saw my wife fly off into the darkness of space. Eventually I saw my beautiful Garrison fly away, until I have a hard time recognizing his face, seeing his smile, or hearing his voice anymore.

You can't break the laws of physics...

No matter how hard you try, you can't keep control over everything...

No matter how hard you try, there are some things that you have no control over...

And no matter how hard you try, it is difficult not to blame yourself for what happened.

Life's spinning, faster and faster…

My grabbing, harder and harder…

My life slipping through my fingers…

Garrison's face, his voice, and his laughter fading from my memory.

Chapter 3:
Evisceration and Emasculation

When asked how I "feel" about losing Garrison, the first two words that come to my mind are evisceration ("to remove the entrails, or to deprive of vital content or force"), and emasculation ("to castrate, geld, or weaken"). I choose to use the term "evisceration" in an emotional context here – where my love, my emotional being, and my happiness were ripped away from deep within me.

My life was ripped apart. I was gutted, to the core. It is like someone reached inside of me, and slowly, deliberately, started pulling my being, my core, and my essence, out from deep within.

I lost my son. I lost my wife. I lost all that was awaiting me in my future. I began placing blame onto myself. I felt totally helpless, and totally alone.

Perspective and memory...

As I write this, I am trying to express how I feel about Garrison's murder, from two perspectives. First of all was my life prior to and immediately after the murder is very much one thing. Trying to express how I feel about it now, is something difficult, in a very different way.

This is so hard for me...

Days Prior to the Murder

Saturday, February 21, 2009.

Two days after Lori discovered the answers to the universe written out on a scroll, we decided take the boys to the beach for a quick visit. It was just supposed to be a nice quiet drive, just to walk around a little bit.

On both the drive there, and on the drive home, she insisted that we listen to audio CD's (of an author which I would not like to give credit to) regarding the relationship between the mind, your life, and your actions. She kept asking me what I thought about what was being said, and how that affects me. A main focus of the audio discussion was on how positive thoughts could generate positive actions, and how you can do what you believe.

When we got to the beach, we took the boys for a walk. Gregory was barely able to walk around, and Garrison was in a stroller. It was a cool day, somewhat overcast. We walked around, looked at birds and plants, played in the sand, and threw rocks. But it was very quiet, and we didn't talk much. Lori was deep in thought, not angry, but seemingly quite content.

We walked back to the truck, and began cleaning up. We discussed going to find some dinner before going home. Lori said she wanted to go to the restroom, and I told her I would watch the boys. However, she ended up being gone for close to two hours.

I was a mess. I had the boys with me in my truck. A couple of times, I parked the truck next to the trail, and walked a little ways to see where she was. I called her phone multiple times. I drove the boys around, and around, in the parking lot, trying to keep them occupied. I drove to adjacent parking lots, thinking that Lori had walked down the path, and that I could meet her.

It was shortly after dark (very dark), and she ended up coming up to the truck, as the beach was closing. I was furious, and she didn't even apologize. She said she wanted to watch the sunset.

The drive home was even quieter. She wanted to listen to the CD again, and I don't remember anything except how upset I was.

What a long, exhausting day…

Sunday, February 22, 2009.

The day prior to Garrison's murder. I was still very emotionally exhausted from the beach trip. To be honest, I don't remember much of what I did that day. I remember that I didn't go anywhere. However, I do remember what Lori did.

She said she wanted to spend the day with Nick and Garrison. She wanted to go on a drive, go shopping, and just have fun. I remember the three of them loading up into the Subaru and leaving me and Gregory for the day.

Lori and I spoke a few times, and it seemed as if she was enjoying herself. However, late that afternoon (or early evening) I received a phone call from Lori. She told me she was at a BMW dealership (specifics excluded intentionally), and told me to give the salesman my personal information, because she was "going to buy" a new car.

I questioned Lori (with passion). I told her that we wouldn't qualify. I told her that financially this would be impossible. She said that everything would be ok.

The salesman got onto the phone. I specifically told him that I did not want to purchase any car, and that I would not be approved for an auto loan. He assured me that there would be no issue.

To make my point, I gave him my information over the phone, with Lori sitting at his side. Prior to hanging up, Lori again assured me that everything was ok.

I was furious. Why the hell is she trying to buy a car? I was embarrassed by the fact that we couldn't, I was furious that she would consider doing this without me. That evening, getting Gregory into bed, was a long miserable night, waiting for them to get home.

I remember hearing a car drive up. I walked to the spare bedroom, to look out towards the street. I saw our car parking, obviously not the BMW. I was shaking, I was so upset. What a wide range of emotions – I was confused, I was relieved, and I was so angry. She didn't have a new car, she didn't get what she wanted, and she made me go through hell during that phone call, and in the hours immediately after.

I was incensed...

I didn't greet them as they came into the house. I was in the master bedroom, sitting by myself on the bed. I heard Lori getting Garrison ready for bed, and the basic rustling of a "normal" life. Then Lori came into the bedroom. She knew I was upset. She sat on the bed next to me. I don't remember saying anything (I probably did, but it wasn't noteworthy). However, I do remember her putting her arms around me, and I (basically) remember what she said to me. I am paraphrasing, but this is what I remember...

"I know this is confusing. I know this doesn't make sense. But this is part of His plan, and everything will be ok. Please trust me, everything will be ok."

Repeated emphasis on "please trust me." "Trust me, it's all going to be ok."

Over, and over, and over, and over...

She kept trying to reassure me that everything would be ok, and that she knew what she was doing, even if it didn't make sense to me.

She left the bedroom, and I tried to go to sleep. I remember being restless, and it took a while to fall asleep. I remember hearing her in the living room and kitchen. I don't remember much else.

My Last Morning with Garrison

Monday morning, February 23, 2009.

This is the day Garrison was murdered, and the day from which I have never fully recovered.

I woke up pretty early. It was still dark. I got up and took a shower, to get ready for school. I had a lecture at 8am, and I had the normal routine of my life. I had to get Gregory ready for school, and if Garrison wasn't asleep, it gave me a little bit of time with him as well.

When I got out of the shower, and as I was getting dressed, I looked at the bed. It looked as if Lori was asleep, but Garrison was sitting upright and looking at me. I remember walking up to him to give him a kiss on the top of the head.

Garrison cried..

Without flinching, Lori yelled at me. She was on the bed, and didn't move a muscle. She was very angry. She just kept saying that I made him cry. It was my "bad energy" which made him upset. It was my "ego" that made him cry. She placed total blame onto me for making Garrison so upset.

I didn't even speak with Lori. It wouldn't have done me any good. I just picked up Garrison to go into the kitchen and make Gregory's lunch.

Funny thing is, the instant I picked up Garrison, he stopped crying.

I walked down the hallway quietly, and took Garrison with me to the kitchen with me for our morning routine. I placed him into his high chair, gave him some Cheerios, turned on the news, and slowly began making Gregory his lunch. I also woke Gregory up, and got him ready for school. The entire time, Garrison was talking (giving it all he had!), and laughing.

The last fond memory of Garrison I have is in that kitchen, that morning. I had picked him up, and was holding him in my left arm. He reached across me with his left hand, pointing at the TV newscast. He said something, with a very serious look on his face. It made me laugh, and we "talked."

I had to leave with Gregory, and go to school.

I took Garrison to his mother...

I walked into the bedroom...

I set Garrison on the bed, and kissed his forehead goodbye, as I have done hundreds of times. He looked up and smiled at me, as he had hundreds of times.

I said good-bye to Lori. She didn't respond to me. She was lying there, on her back, with her arms draped over her face, covering her eyes. She was saying something – more like chanting something.

All I heard was this droning voice as I walked away, down the hall, never knowing that I had said my last goodbye to Garrison, and that I would never see him alive again...

That day didn't go well for me. I was very tired, having not slept very well the previous night. My morning didn't start off well either, being yelled at, and seeing Lori not respond to me was troublesome.

I called multiple times during the day, but as often happed, she didn't respond.

The last time I remember calling her was to let her know I was coming home, and asking if she wanted me to pick up anything for the family.

No answer...

Coming Home from Work

I remember that I was done at school about 5pm or so, and I picked up Gregory from RCC's ECS program, as usual. I got home around 545 or 6pm. Everything seemed usual, albeit very quiet, when I walked into the house.

Except Nick was sitting on the couch in the living room, and he looked upset.

As we walked in, Gregory ran up to give his big brother a hug, but Nick didn't respond at all. He just sat there, looking forward towards the television set.

Nick had spent the entire weekend with us, and it was my understanding that Lori was going to take him back to his dad's house that morning, so that he could go to school. I didn't know that she had kept him home that day, until I came into the front door. He had been having a lot of conflict with Lori lately as well, generally dumb teenage stuff like Nick wanting to spend all of his time on his cell phone, being totally self-absorbed, and being disrespectful. So I just figured Lori wanted to spend the day with him. When I walked into the front door, seeing him upset, I just thought that it was more of the same tension between him and his mother.

I asked Nick what was going on, but I assumed that I already knew. I thought that Lori was very angry, and they had a bad day together. So I tried to make small talk, trying to get Nick to open up a bit and let me know what was going on. From my perspective, his resistance in speaking to me about it was just more examples of the tension between him and his mother. He generally didn't want to talk very much. I thought that this was just more of the same. As usual, I tried to get him to open up a bit, and to see things from a different perspective.

I asked if he had eaten, and I asked if he would like for me to make them some dinner. He said yes.

I asked him if he thought his mother would like something to eat. He said she didn't want to be disturbed.

I went into the kitchen, and made both Nick and Gregory dinner. I remember specifically what I made – grilled hamburger patties, sliced tomato, cottage cheese, bread with butter, and glasses of milk.

I remember not eating, not even making myself anything to eat, because I was pretty upset. As I was preparing the meal for my boys, there was a lot of tension evident with Nick, and this just seemed to continue the feelings I had from the entire weekend, and especially that morning. I came home once again to a house filled with angst, and there wasn't anything I could do. Lori had separated herself, with Garrison, to the other side of the house. From my perspective, I felt that she did this because she was still mad at me, and didn't want to be near me.

As I served the boys, I sat down in the living room with them. I asked Nick if he was ok, and he said yes. I asked him if he would like to talk, and he said no. I asked about his mother, and whether he thought I should go back and talk with her. Nick strongly reiterated that she didn't want to be disturbed, and that the door was closed.

I thought that I should go back and talk with her. I thought that I needed to let her vent, to let her speak her mind – anything to restore some feeling of normality within our home.

"Mom's in a bad place." Nick said this with a blank stare, and with little emotion. He looked exhausted. He said over and over that she didn't want to be disturbed. I asked whether he knew if she was upset with me, and he said yes. I asked if he thought that if I left the house, would she come out and spend time with them, and again he said yes.

So I left my house... with Nick and Gregory eating on the couch, naively thinking that if I left the house for a while, that Lori and the boys could relax a bit.

I left my house...

My murdered son's cold body was lying in my bedroom. My psychotic wife was in the bathroom.

I left my house...

I left my two boys, sitting in the living room. I left them defenseless, I left them alone, and I left Nick at a time when he was so utterly alone in his own private prison.

I left my house, because I was so ignorant to what had happened.

I left my house, because I didn't want to be in that depressing atmosphere, nor did I want to be around Lori.

I left my house, like I had never done before.

I left my house...

Finding Garrison

I didn't know what to do. I wasn't very hungry, I knew I couldn't "think" very well so going back to school to grade wouldn't work, so I decided to do something I hadn't done since Lori and I had first met.

Go to a movie...

I got to the theater about 710pm or so, and the only movie that was coming up was *"Taken"*, starring Liam Neeson. It was a good movie, and it got my mind off my troubles for a while.

Imagine how I feel about seeing a movie called *"Taken"* now...

The movie was over a little after 9pm, and I thought it was still too early to go home. I honestly had hoped to get home after the boys had gone to sleep. Perhaps Lori would be up, and we could talk – perhaps not (which would have been preferable). It was evident that she hadn't wanted to speak with me the entire day, so I didn't know what to expect.

So instead of going directly home, I went to Starbucks close to our home, and sat down for a coffee. I also read the day's newspaper. I just sat there, being quiet, and being mindless. Later, I looked up, and noticed that the staff was cleaning up, getting ready to close, so I got ready to go home.

I got home shortly after 10pm. I unlocked the door, and quietly walked in. There sat Nick, and Gregory, on the couch, in the same positions as when I left.

I thought to myself "what the hell... it's past Gregory's bedtime!"

As I walked in, Nick looked at me, and his face had a look that my words can't describe. He looked distraught, scared and very tired. I asked him if he was ok...

"I think my mom did something bad." The look on his face was hard to describe...

"What do you mean?" I asked.

"I think mom hurt Garrison." My heart stopped...

"What?"

"I think mom killed Garrison..."

I was numb. To be honest, I don't think I believed him, at least for a split second. I turned to walk down the hallway, towards the master bedroom. I remember Nick frantically yelling "please don't hurt my mom!" as I walked away.

The main hallway was dark. It was long. There was an attached hallway, to the right, which led directly into the master bedroom. As I walked through that hallway, with the deep sickening realization that something was truly terribly wrong, I don't recall then wondering to myself whether Nick was mistaken. I don't remember thinking that Garrison would be ok.

I sadly knew what I would find...

Have you ever seen those movies, where the director tries to convey a feeling of hopelessness while someone is walking down a hallway? Where the end of the hallway "squeezes" away from the actor? What a difficult feeling of helplessness to try to show visually.

Those directors are pretty good at what they do.

I finally reached the end of the hallway, and I opened the door to the bedroom. I called out Lori's name. No answer, just darkness and silence.

I walked into the master bedroom, and heard the shower running in the bathroom to the right. Even with its door closed, I noticed that the light was off in the bathroom.

I looked towards my left and saw the bed, with the comforter in a large pile. I looked straight ahead and saw a large red stain on the floor...

My heart stopped.

At this point, I don't recall hearing Nick, Gregory, the shower or anything else. I was emotionally numb, but in a strange way I was also thinking rationally. I slowly side-stepped around the blood, walked towards my left, in a circular motion, stepping in front of the bed, slowly reached down with my left hand, and lifted the comforter.

There laid my beautiful son. It was Garrison, and then it was not. He was so still. I knew instantly...

I reached down, ever so gently, and with my right hand open-palmed, I touched his chest.

It was cold to the touch – like touching a cool table top. I will never forget that sensation on my hand.

His abdomen had been penetrated, and his intestines were exposed. I can never forget that visual sensation in my mind.

I was so afraid of touching anything, and I remember thinking "this is a crime scene.... Be careful!" How stupid. To my core I regret the fact that I didn't even pick Garrison up, in order to give him a final hug. But there I was, seemingly "thinking" rationally.

I turned my head, over my left shoulder, looking towards the bathroom. The door was closed, the shower was still running, and the lights were turned off.

I slowly backed away from the bed, and walked towards the bathroom door. I put my hand on the door handle, and slowly tried to open it, but it was locked.

I stood there, wondering what to do. I wanted to kick down that fucking door, and get to where Lori was. I began to bang my fist on the door. Still no answer. I yelled for Lori, and still, no answer.

In my heart, I knew she was dead as well. I just knew that she had killed Garrison, went into the shower, slit her wrists, and bled to death.

In my mind I had realized that I had lost both Lori and Garrison that day.

Funny... in retrospect, I did.

Then an interesting thought occurred to me. I also knew if I kicked down the door, I would have to fix it. Now I think to myself "to hell with that door!" But, during that moment, I was convinced that I had lost Lori as well, and there wasn't a "need" to bust into the bathroom. So instead, I decided to pick the lock instead.

It is funny how your mind works, at different times, in different situations. My thoughts seemed perfectly reasonable to me...

I felt like a zombie, walking back through the hallway, walking right past Gregory and Nick. I don't recall looking over towards them. I think I told them to stay put, but to be honest I don't remember. I walked through the kitchen, and into the garage, where I got a small screwdriver – one small enough that I knew that would be able to pick a bathroom door lock. I again walked back towards the bathroom where Lori was. This time I do remember yelling with force at Nick to stay put, however I don't remember what he said to me. He was saying something, and he was very upset. I don't remember Gregory sitting there, at all.

I went back to the bathroom door, banged on it with my fists once again, and still received no reply. I reached down and picked the lock in an instant, and slowly opened the door. I said "Lori," and still no answer. I was already prepared to find her cold body in the shower.

I reached to the left with my hand, and turned on the light. A split second later, I noticed a sudden movement instantly to my right. This caused my body to go onto high alert again (that good old sympathetic nervous system). Looking towards the shower, I couldn't see her body. The shower glass was clouded, to where you could see an "image" but not any of the detail. To me, at that moment, it was like she was in a fog. However, her hand was touching the shower door glass, and I could see that with vivid detail. That image haunts me.

My heart stopped, and I gasped.

She wasn't dead...

My emotions, and my state of energy and awareness, had been, and were continuing to be, on a roller coaster.

I went from a zombie-like numbness walking down the hallway, to being filled with incredible amounts of dread and sadness, to being very cognizant and aware of every move that I carefully made at a crime scene, to being ready to go to war with the murderer of my son, to incredible sadness at the "realization" that I had lost both my son and my wife, back on "battle" mode, and the very real possibility that now that she was "discovered," Lori could choose to attack me.

The entirety in the range of my emotions, and the absolute reality of the situation kept slapping me in the face, and punching me in the gut. I was breathless. I was very aware. I was lost.

Trembling with controlled rage, I stepped back away from where she was sitting...

I was giving myself a little bit of "space" between me and her. I didn't know what to expect.

Reaching forward, with my left hand, I slowly slid the shower door open with my left hand (away from me, and sliding it towards her). There she sat, naked, sitting in a stream of cold water. This was a woman I didn't recognize. She had a blank, evil, unrecognizable stare, looking deep into my eyes. If ever there was an example of a "soulless" expression on someone's face, I was now witness.

Thinking back, I fully expected her to leap at my face – like *Gollum* going for "the ring"...

I was angry, and fully prepared to go to physical battle with what was my wife. I remember thinking she will never hurt anyone, ever, again.

In as calm a voice as my strength could muster, "Lori, what happened?"

Nothing. No reaction at all. Just that blank, soulless stare.

It seemed like an eternity, but I am sure that it was just a brief moment...

Lori slowly raised her left hand, slowly taking it up towards the shower door, placing her palm onto the door, to slowly close the door, all the time with her eyes fixated upon mine.

A deep, unwavering, ambivalent, grotesquely impassionate stare...

I lost my wife.

This woman sitting in the shower was not my wife. I could not recognize her anymore.

How ironic.

Closing that shower door, in the manner that she did, had tremendous meaning to me. She visually divided her face from mine, creating a physical barrier between us, as if shutting the door was a final climactic step, separating her life from mine.

This woman I didn't recognize anymore just dismissed me, in the most impassionate way.

I slowly stepped back. I was in shock. Had she attacked me at that moment, my guard was down – her attack would have initially been successful. Fortunately, she didn't. I turned around, and numbingly looked straight ahead. I stared towards the closet. Then a thought entered my mind…

My shotgun is sitting there. In that instant, I wanted nothing more than to blow her head off.

What a strange thought. Many would think it righteous and acceptable; I do as well, but not in that instant. I remember thinking about that shotgun and pulling out my cell phone. I pondered what to do. Suddenly, I said to myself "fuck you, Lori."

I wanted her in prison. I wanted her to suffer in her mind's prison. I wanted her to pay for what she did. I also realized that had I removed her head with a shotgun blast, I would be in jail.

All I could think about was Gregory.

At that moment, what focused me is my wanting to protect the boys. I feared her attacking them…

I retreated down the hall, towards where Gregory and Nick were standing. Nick was frantically crying. Gregory looked so scared. He didn't have a clue what was going on.

I had to call for help, but my main concern was for the boys' safety. I took the boys into another bedroom, shut the door, and had them lock it. I told Nick not to unlock it, except for me. I was still afraid Lori would come out of the shower and attack them.

In hindsight it was a mistake, but I called Nick's father first. I tried to explain what happened, and I told him he needed to come get Nick. Then I dialed 911. I stupidly thought that Nick's dad could get him out of there before the police could get there.

The 911 operator kept me on the phone until the police arrived.

The Arrest

The Riverside City Police arrived at my home. I don't know how long it took them, but it didn't seem that long. I was still on the phone with the 911 operator. I remember just wanting to turn off the damn phone, and sit down. I was irritated at the operator for talking at me the way she did. However, in retrospect I realize that she was doing precisely what she should have been doing – keeping me pre-occupied, and trying to keep some measure of "control," over this uncontrolled situation.

The police were at my door. I recall that it was either two or three police officers. I don't know exactly what was said, or how. A lot of the "fine detail" has escaped my memory. They came in, and I pointed down the hall, to where Garrison's body would be found. They walked down the hall towards the bedroom, towards my son's body, and towards what used to be Lori.

During this time I moved the boys back into the living room, and Nick became hysterical. He was sobbing, and pleading with the police not to hurt his mother. He didn't want to see her arrested. Seeing Nick this way was very difficult for me, but it was more difficult seeing little Gregory. The fear on his face, because of the activity, the sounds, the energy, and Nick's actions just were too much for my three year old son.

I ran over to where they were crouched on the floor. The only thought on my mind was to protect them, and I wrapped my body around both of theirs, covering them, and shielding them. I remember one of the police officers was standing at my side, but I wasn't paying attention to him.

Then, suddenly, the sounds from the bathroom began...

There were forceful, very loud, and directive voices from the police. I heard wrestling, fighting, and shouting. Lori was resisting arrest from within the shower. Lori reached for a policeman's gun, and the police responded as such.

The energy of the moment was absolutely intense. The sounds that were created by this energy were indeed deafening, and there was a tremendous swirl of activity.

I know that a lot of this energy was also created by Nick's hysterics, and by Gregory's cries. But my ability to remember precisely what was happening is difficult.

Then... quiet.

When the energy levels of the moment subsided, I looked up, and there were police everywhere. The numbers grew from two or three to literally dozens, and I had no idea when it happened. Wave after wave of police came in through the door. Back and forth through the front door they went. Back and forth from the hallway into and out from the bedroom. They were constantly hovering over me and my sons.

Eventually, the police escorted Lori down the hall towards the living room, where we were located. She was in a white bathrobe, and her hair was still wet. I glanced up, and saw her face, but I don't think she noticed me. As the line of police escorting Lori walked towards me, I was sickened in my stomach, and turned my back towards her as she walked past. I couldn't bear to look at her.

She said something. I don't recall what it was, and I don't care what it was.

When she wasn't in the house anymore, I remember being able to look around, and absorb what was happening, with more detail in my recollection. I distinctly remember the absolute sadness on the faces of the police officers. I remember that they couldn't look me in the eye, and kept avoiding my gaze. I remember wishing that someone would come up, and tell me everything was ok, and that everything would be ok. I remember that some of these fine police officers had tears in their eyes, and very solemn expressions on their faces. I remember how deafening silent it was in that room, and I remember how alone I felt.

I can't imagine what goes through someone's mind in moments like this. Police and firefighters are trained professionals, continuously trained for almost every situation. But, how could any training prepare them for this. I found out years later that many of the police had received some counseling after this evening. I have no idea if it is standard practice, or if it was of their own choice, but either way I am glad that there are support mechanisms for these brave men and women.

About a year after Garrison died, I learned something else that was quite disturbing to me. I was talking with a mother of a child who was with Gregory at RCC's ECS center. She admitted something, which in actuality was very saddening to me. Her husband is a paramedic, and he responded to the murder. Evidently, on the way to my home, he was under the impression that it was Gregory who was murdered. He was under the impression that he would find this child, who had grown up with his child. He was under the impression that he would have to take care of the body, of a child whom he had been witness to his laughter, his playing on the playground, and his smiles. I could not imagine what went through that poor man's mind, as he drove up to the crime scene. I also could not imagine what went through that poor man's mind, as he realized what actually happened, and to whom...

There the three of us sat, in that house, where my son's cold body was found. I don't recall how long we were there, after the police arrived. I don't remember all of my conversations. There were questions posed to me, and there were people everywhere. I remember police trying to console Nick, but I can't remember what happened.

It seemed like such a long time – I had an idea of what they were doing, and why. It was excruciating just sitting there.

As I sit here trying to write down my thoughts and memories, I can't even remember Gregory during this time, nor what was happening to him...

But I do remember what happened next. I began to panic. I pleaded with the police to make sure Garrison was indeed dead, and please check again to see if he was breathing. In my mind I knew he was dead, but I had hoped beyond hope that he was still barely alive.

I remember, as I pleaded for them to double-check, the look on the face of the police officer. How idiotic I sounded to myself, how pathetic I must have seemed to him, and how sad the entirety of the situation in reality was…

At this time I was standing next to both Nick and Gregory, and the police officer put his hand on my shoulder. His hand was gentle, but firm, and it was shaking. He whispered into my ear "I must place these handcuffs on you. Please, do not resist me."

I remember thinking about how upsetting this must be to him, and how much I felt for him.

I also didn't have the will to fight. I was emotionally beaten, and physically exhausted.

I replied "I understand."

That is how I was taken into custody. They escorted me to a police car, and placed me into the back seat. There were people everywhere, and there were lights everywhere. There was a swirl of activity, all around me. There was yellow flagging all around the crime scene. There were neighbors standing around, trying to find out what happened. Cars were driving onto our street, only to be turned away.

Just like you see on television…

I was in that car well over an hour. I was just sitting there, handcuffed, shoeless, and cold. The most miserable, uncomfortable seat, not enough room for my legs, and my knees pushed up toward my chest and chin. Sitting there was physically uncomfortable, and emotionally torturous. The longer I sat there, the more I just wanted to sit and hug Gregory. I felt so helpless, and I also began to panic. I remember my body "swelling," my fists and arms straining against my handcuffs. As I became more and more uncomfortable, I remember telling myself, over and over – "breathe, just breathe…" I tried to calm myself down by closing my eyes and breathing. After quite a while, I did calm down a little bit.

Until they walked Gregory and Nick past the police car I was in.

I cried out their names. Nick looked around, but he didn't see me. I don't think Gregory heard me. It didn't matter how loud I yelled anyways. There was nothing I could do. All I wanted to do was to talk to them, to hold them, and to tell them I loved them.

I couldn't do any of that. I was a suspect in a child's murder, in my own child's murder. My wife had just murdered my son. I found my dead son's body. I found my psychotic wife in a cold stream of water, sitting in the shower. I was now sitting in the back of a police car watching my son and my stepson being escorted away by the police.

At that moment, I didn't know if I would ever see them again…

I watched as they passed my car, and looked over my shoulder. A crowd had gathered, behind the crime scene tape. There was Nick's father, having arrived after my phone call, looking absolutely distraught. I felt for him, and I wonder what he was thinking.

A police officer came and opened the car door. I was elated. I thought I could finally see my boys.

"Where is your car seat?" He asked in a very cold, uncaring, and dispassionate voice. I wondered if he had been inside the house, and had seen my sons' body. How could he be so callous to me!

I told him that it was in my pickup truck, and that my keys were in my left pocket. He made me stand up, in order to get the keys. I told him I was cold, would like my pair of shoes, and I wanted to see my family.

He didn't say another word. He placed me back into the police car, went to the front, and turned up the heater on high for me. I was thankful. At least in that moment.

I watched as he went to my pickup truck, opened it up, and got out the car seat. I then watched as he walked to a police car behind me, and watched him struggle to place the car seat into that police car. One of my last memories of this evening, at that house, was Gregory in the arms of another police officer, with his arms resting around his neck, being helped into the car seat. I remember hoping that Gregory would trust the police, and not panic. I also remember being so proud of him. He seemed so brave to me.

As I sat there, I again became uncomfortable. I was indeed thankful that the police officer had turned up the heat, because I was cold (undoubtedly I was in shock). But now I realized that he intentionally left me with the heater on, full blast, with all of the windows closed. Now I was sitting in an oven, handcuffed. I went from being stressed out about not being able to see my boys, being very cold and uncomfortable, to now sweating and being uncomfortable. I prefer to think my being uncomfortable was unintentional. It is also entirely possible that the police in actuality didn't know exactly what had happened, and they were intentionally making me extremely uncomfortable, as part of their strategy to determine the truth. This was definitely a form of psychological warfare, making someone realize the full extent of not being in control, of any part of their lives.

For some reason I also recall seeing Lori being escorted to another police car. I am not sure why, or how, this happened. But the vision of her in handcuffs and being led across my driveway is quite vivid.

So there I sat. The culmination of an excruciating day, sitting by myself, uncomfortably numb, my life as I knew it ripped apart.

I was totally helpless.

The term evisceration is generally used when removing the internal organs during slaughter. The term emasculation generally refers to the castration of a male. I use these descriptive terms in a different way...

My life was eviscerated that day. Everything that I thought, everything that I had hoped, everything that I knew was ripped apart, and torn away.

I felt totally emasculated. I had no control over what had happened, and no control for what my life had in store for me. I feared that it would be felt that I played a role in Garrison's death. I feared that I would never see my son Gregory again. I feared that I would lose my job. I feared I would spend my life in prison. I feared that somehow, someway, through Lori's control and manipulation that I would be blamed for Garrison's death, and I was so scared.

I sat in that police car, eviscerated and emasculated.

I could do nothing.

And I knew it.

I was powerless, and I realized that Lori was still in control. She had begun this new chapter of our lives by murdering our son, Garrison, leaving me as a suspect unable to care for Gregory or Nick in their time of need. Now my immediate life was out of my hands.

I guess this wasn't that different than before Garrison's murder. To some extent, Lori was still in control…

How interesting, thinking about that drive home from the beach. Lori listening to a self-help CD, emphasizing that positive thoughts could change the universe. Emphasizing the power of the mind, and how this power needs to be harnessed.

Perhaps Lori could not control her thoughts, which would bring into question whether she really had any power. Perhaps Lori thought that she was totally in control over her thoughts. However, her thoughts (positive?), and the power of her mind, still did not keep her from doing what she did. Perhaps this is precisely what she wanted all along.

To set Garrison free?

I will never know…

Lori eviscerated Garrison, physically. Lori eviscerated me as well, metaphorically speaking.

She ripped my son away, she ripped my life apart, and she ripped what I thought was a secure life away from me.

Lori emasculated me. I was not in control of her, I had no control over Garrison's health and welfare, I had no control over what she did, and I had no control over my life anymore.

Evisceration and emasculation.

Two very humbling realizations...

Chapter 4:
Focus

I call this chapter Focus, and I think it adequately describes what happened in the days immediately following Garrison's death, up until when the trial ended. In many respects, I feel that this is one of the most important chapters in this book.

Garrison's death not only impacted my life, and the lives of those who immediately surrounded me, but it also had a tremendous impact on my community. As I have mentioned, in one example Garrison's death was the "final straw" for a group of dedicated professionals to finally come together to form the *Inland Empire Perinatal Mental Health Collaborative*. This group had been coming together long before Garrison's death, but this tragedy finally spurred them into formal action.

I think the value of this chapter is in how I dealt with this tragedy – how I functionally made it, living life, coping with my new reality, day by excruciating day. This is compared with, what I think, is the value of Chapter 2 (Centrifugal Force), where I attempt to describe my life spinning out of control, prior to the murder. This is also compared with the value of Chapter 5 (CRI), where I try to understand, and put into perspective, all of the missing links which were indeed the warning signs that I may have missed which led to Garrison's murder.

Collectively, I believe that the messages I am trying to impart – identifying how my life was falling apart, how I dealt with the daily reality of my tragedy, and reflections upon what I may have missed, are the most value to the reader for this entire endeavor – if indeed they are interested in learning from my experiences.

This is quite long, and I have tried to organize my focus into a few categories:

- My focus being in custody, and being investigated.

- My focus during the realization that I have a new situational reality.

- My focus on the psychological needs of Gregory, Nicholas, and myself.

- My focus in being strong for my family, my friends, and my colleagues.

- My focus on how I attempted to deal with Lori's family and friends.

- My focus during the actual trial, and the public arena.

- My focus in dealing with Garrison's murderer.

- My victims impact statement during the sentencing hearing.

Each of these areas of emphasis presented me with unique problems, issues, and various ways in which I tried (successfully and unsuccessfully) to find resolution. With each of these, I tried to "focus" on what was important with my "eye on the prize" for the conclusion of this journey. Eventually, I knew in my heart, the end of my journey would be to rebuild a life with my surviving son Gregory, and begin to rediscover some "normalcy" every day. I always thought that if I was patient enough, that I could stabilize, normalize, and solidify my life again.

At least, that is what *my* focus consistently remained…

Along this journey, I have made many, many mistakes. I wish I could have done so many things differently. Many decisions were made when I don't feel that I was thinking straight. Many decisions were made when I was extremely emotional, and quite simply exhausted.

However, I do feel that I did everything that I could under these unbearable circumstances, and for this I have no regrets.

My Focus – Being in Custody and the Investigation

It was a very quiet ride to the police station. It was surreal, extremely lonely, and with a tremendous weight - my realization of the reality of the moment was staggering…

I don't remember much from it. There were various stimuli, lights, smells, and sounds on the police radio. I just stared out the window blindly, and my numbness was overbearing. When we pulled into the parking lot of the police station I thought to myself "funny, I didn't know this was here." I had driven by that particular station multiple times, but never had thought about its significance.

It is no longer unknown to me, as I drive by.

I had been placed, in custody, in the back of a police car. When the car drove away from my house, I remember looking over my left shoulder, towards this house where Garrison's body remained. Lots of lights, and lots of activity. It was like I was driving away from a part of my life, in a manner in which I had no control – I wasn't in the "driver's seat" anymore. Even though we left in a caravan of activity, it seemed as if we were all alone during the drive to the police station. Reality hit again as we pulled into the station – immediately we were surrounded by a lot of activity.

The car I was riding in slowly drove, and turned left, into a parking spot. As we drove towards the station building, I suddenly saw Lori, being taken from her car into the access door of the station. Same bath robe, hands cuffed behind her back, two or three police officers escorting her, and I remember thinking that she looked so "business-like."

She didn't appear to be upset, at all…

You often see, at least on television, people who have been involved in shootings or violence. Often they appear unfazed, nonchalant, and even disassociated or distant.

It is almost as if it is not a "big deal" at all.

Then, in an instant, she was gone behind the door…

I didn't know that this would be the last time I would see her for over two years.

I was still handcuffed, and I was escorted into what appeared to me an office lobby, with multiple cubicles where people could work at their computer stations.

It was very quiet, with very few people there. It must have been just after midnight. I would have expected a normal amount of hustling and bustling, but in reality didn't see any of it. No bars. No screaming drug addicts in custody. I saw nothing that would overtly indicate this was a police station. It was quiet, and I felt very cold, and quite alone. I observed many stares in my direction.

I was led into a room about 10 feet by 20 feet or so. I remember it had a small table, chairs, quite a lot of floor space, with a small couch and a coffee table. I am thankful that it wasn't a bar-laden holding cell.

When the police escorted me into this room, they were very quiet, and efficient. They couldn't (or wouldn't) answer questions about Gregory and Nick. They deposited me into this room, and closed the door. I kept trying to tell myself to relax, but at times it was unbearable. I could hear distant voices. I remember how cold I was; my shoeless feet were extremely cold. It seems as if I spent hours pacing in circles around the room. I was trying to keep moving because of my stress, and I was trying to keep moving because I was cold – very cold.

No one came in to see me. No one came in to see how I was doing. I was alone, in the excruciating timeless prison within my mind.

Eventually my pacing to keep my mind occupied and my body warm turned into a feeble attempt to keep from evacuating my bladder where I stood. I was physically miserable, emotionally exhausted, and I didn't know what to do. It is no exaggeration that eventually I couldn't take it anymore. I quietly knocked on the door, and backed away from the door's entrance.

A police officer opened the door, with two others immediately behind him. I asked for permission to use the restroom. The officer closed the door, and came back a few minutes later.

I was re-handcuffed, and escorted to their restroom, I noticed people stopped talking as I entered the room. Most (if not all) glanced up in my direction, but I tried not to look at any of them. I needed to get to the restroom, and I didn't want to look in their eyes. It also seems as if they didn't want to look into mine, as well. They seemed sad, and uncomfortable.

Perhaps this is my wanting them to be sad, and uncomfortable.

But how could anyone, no matter how "bitter" they become on the job, become so dispassionate in the face of such tragedy?

I prefer to think that they actually cared...

The door to the restroom was opened, and I was allowed to walk in. It was a "normal" restroom you would expect in an office atmosphere. However, I was handcuffed. I felt so stupid, having to turn around and ask what to do, not knowing the "etiquette" of prisoner restroom behavior. I didn't know if he would take the handcuffs off of me. I didn't know if I would be allowed to urinate myself, if the police had to "assist" me, or some awkward combination of both.

I was told that I could have one handcuff taken off. The policeman removed the cuff from my right hand only. I was then allowed to relieve myself, but with the police officer standing there.

This was extremely awkward. In page one of the "guy rules," it is typed in bold type that in a restroom you don't speak to another man, you don't occupy a urinal next to someone (when there are others available), and you never, ever, stare.

So much for the "guy rules"...

Upon finishing in the restroom, I was again handcuffed, and taken back into the waiting room. I have no idea when I again saw someone. It was literally hours, but eventually two detectives came into the room.

When they came in, it was in that moment, that reality hit me again. I could see the looks on their faces, and they expressed their condolences and assured me that both Nick and Gregory were fine. These were the first caring, compassionate words I had heard since I discovered Garrison's body seven or eight hours earlier.

They informed me that I was no longer a suspect. I even think they turned up the heat in the room for me. They sat down in two small chairs next to the coffee table, allowing me to sit on the small couch directly across from them.

We had a long conversation, most of which I don't recall. They had many questions about the evening, my coming home, my going to the movies, and coming home again. We discussed Nick's words, his actions, my actions in discovering Garrison's body, my actions in finding Lori alive, and my actions afterward.

I was being interrogated, and de-briefed, at the same time.

The detectives were trying to get a full account of the evening, especially from my perspective. My going to the movies that night was extremely odd (to me, and to them I am sure), and eventually became a focus in my testimony during Lori's murder trial, especially from the defense council perspective. It must have seemed so odd, so coincidently out-of-character for me to "magically" leave on the same evening that Garrison had died. Admittedly, that seemed quite strange for me as well, trying to explain what had happened.

There were two areas of inquiry which we spoke about for quite a long time.

The Shotgun

The first "odd" area of conversation dealt with my shotgun. This was the gun in which I had briefly considered using upon her, when I found Lori sitting naked in the cold shower. I distinctly remember looking at my closet and thinking about it. When they asked me where my shotgun was, I told them it was in the closet. They challenged me, saying no, it wasn't.

I was dazed, and I was confused...

After contemplation, I said that I remember it being in the closet. I did say that perhaps I didn't remember correctly, and if it wasn't in the closet, it had to be in the garage, next to a pistol that I had stored there (along with their ammunition).

Again, they challenged me (sternly) and said, no it wasn't...

I was completely confused now. And I was also very flustered.

They asked why my shotgun was in my truck.

"My truck?" I asked. I was totally in shock. My mind reeled with what was happening. They clarified themselves, saying that it wasn't in the truck I drove every day, but that the shotgun was found in the bed of my other pickup. I emphasized that I had no idea why or how the shotgun was found in my truck.

Then I had a gut feeling of why. All of a sudden, at least in my mind, it all made sense. At least it made sense, to me.

I honestly believe that Lori moved the shotgun before I got home. I think that she feared what I might do. A light bulb went off in my mind. I believe that she feared that once I discovered what she had done, that there would be major retribution or retaliation, and that she didn't want me exacting my revenge upon her with my shotgun.

In my mind, this meant that she had carefully planned what she did, even to the last details.

There was forethought, there was fear of the inevitable, and there was a distinct thought-process. I have always thought this was huge, legally speaking, in her case. I am still convinced of this.

Gregory E. Burchett

The Garden in the Garage

The second area of concern, which led to a lot of questions and discussion, dealt with what they found in the garage. Or more importantly, what they didn't find. As I mentioned earlier in Chapter 2, Lori had begun to consume a lot of marijuana. So much so, that it became a financial burden on our family. This is when she obtained a medical marijuana card, and she had found a "marijuana collective" in Orange County, in order to make her medical marijuana purchases.

Just to re-emphasize, she felt that the marijuana was a perfect way for her to self-treat her anger. She had major anger issues, and the pot helped her to, as she put it, take the "edge off."

She began consuming so much, that we started having discussions on whether to grow it ourselves. It would solve our problem of spending substantial money for Lori, and we were assured that we could sell some back to the collective as well.

So Lori brought home a few small seedlings, on a couple of different occasions. We began growing them, but it became quite evident (quickly) that I would have to get serious about their care. I was also very concerned about keeping this "venture" secret.

So we agreed that I should build a small greenhouse in the garage. We used PVC irrigation pipe for a frame, purchased some black plastic liner to make the sides, and put in a mercury vapor lamp, as the source of light.

It was working wonderfully, and the plants were thriving. The night the police arrived they were about 18 inches tall. We had yet to harvest any of this "crop."

Missing The Links

And I was scared to death. I feared that in addition to Garrison being murdered, Gregory would be taken away from me, because of those stupid plants.

I panicked.

While I was on the phone with the 911 operator, and the boys were locked in the other bedroom, I managed to walk into the garage, grab a large trash bag, and throw away all of the plants.

Again, not thinking straight, I left the greenhouse where it stood. So my efforts really didn't matter.

So the questioning obviously focused on what we were doing in the garage. Without hesitation, I explained everything to the detectives. I even told them where I had thrown the plants away.

Evidently they had not known this. I observed on television footage that actually showed the police taking the trash bag out of my trash can, the following day. Evidently my "tip" helped them find what they were looking for.

They asked if I had been smoking the pot. I said no.

Of course, based on their facial expression, I doubt they believed me, until I raised my right arm in the air and said "pull my blood."

Then they believed me.

Scientific evidence is wonderful, if you have nothing to hide.

Later that morning, they informed me that the marijuana would not be an issue for me personally. They did say, however, that child protective services may wish to speak to me about the marijuana and the shotgun.

They did wish to speak to me...

Multiple times.

The Reunion

After our lengthy discussion, somewhere around 530am, I was finally escorted to see my two boys. I was led into the lobby of the main offices, walked down and through another door, into what appeared to be a conference room. Walking through the door, I looked straight ahead, and saw Nick sitting there in a chair, next to a table. He was talking with an officer. I turned and looked to the right, and there was Gregory. He was lying there, asleep, looking so peaceful, on the floor. He was on a blanket, covered in another blanket, his head was resting on a pillow, and he was completely surrounded by stuffed animals and toys. What a sense of relief. Instantly I was at ease. Seeing him there brought some measure of peace and tranquility to my heart.

But then I glanced again towards Nick. I remember the look on his face. I saw his anguish, his pain, and his despair. He looked exhausted, and he looked beat down. I won't ever forget that look. At that moment he hadn't noticed me.

I can't remember any of our conversations that morning. We hugged and cried. Nick seemed so distant, emotionally, as if he was in a fog.

I am sure I was in a fog, as well.

Missing The Links

The police said that they would escort me back to my house. I remember having to wait until Nick's father arrived at the police station, to pick him up. I was surprised that he wasn't already there, when we were released. I would have been banging down the door to get to Nick, but that is just my opinion. I don't recall speaking with Nick's father too much, just wanting to get Nick safe. It was a very surreal experience early that morning.

In hindsight, I wish Nick would have stayed with me that day, and for a couple of days after that. But, realistically, he needed to be with his dad. Had he been with me though, he would have been in therapy instantly. That, however, is another story.

We finally left about 630am. A friendly Riverside City police officer drove me and Gregory back to the house where Garrison's mother murdered him. The house was surrounded by police and the news media. Unfortunately, I was not allowed to enter my house. I needed clothing for both of us. I needed to brush my teeth. I wanted a hot shower, a long soaking steam filled hot shower, so bad. But, I couldn't get into the house. I didn't even have shoes. I had to ask permission for a police officer, for someone to go into the house and get me some shoes.

I felt so pathetic. I felt so helpless – just like over the last 15 hours.

As I sit here, trying to remember how I felt, it was very surrealistic. Gregory and I were driven to our house in the police car, and as we arrived, there was a tremendous amount of activity taking place. Police detectives and patrol officers, fire fighters, ambulance drivers, and the media were surrounding my home like scavengers descending on a carcass.

All of this seemed like it was still the previous night…

I was numb…

Trying to get clothes for Gregory, or even something as simple as some shoes for myself, was in my mind a slap in my face with reality. I wasn't allowed into my home. I had to get permission to get my shoes? Absolutely. I needed clothes for Gregory? Not even a possibility. The police did escort me back to my house from jail, but it wasn't my house anymore – it was a crime scene.

I was facing a new situation now, and I had to deal with it. I was supposed to go to work, in order to give a biology lecture to over 100 students at 8am. Gregory should have been at daycare by 7am at the latest. What do I do now?

My Focus – A New Situational Reality

Tuesday, February 24, 2009 – the morning after Garrison's murder. This was the first day of the rest of my life, one which will never be the same. I refer to this new day, and my new life, as my new "situational reality." After being driven home I then sat in front of this house, this disgusting scene of this disgusting crime.

We were dropped off. It felt as if we were dumped off.

I was now supposed to "go on with my day," and I had no idea what to do. I remember feeling that I was being "delivered" by the police, and I had no one there, no one to help me, no one to even give me a hug.

I had no one to tell me *what I needed to do*.

You watch movies or television, and you see prisoners being "pushed" out the door from prison, and no one is there waiting for them. What a great visual message.

I felt *that* alone.

I was now placed into a very unfamiliar situation, one which I was never expecting, nor a situation that I was fully prepared for. What possibly can I do?

Reality Check #1 – Get Gregory Safe

I had to think straight. Concentrate – first things first. What is my first situational reality? Getting Gregory to RCC's ECS program and daycare center.

My getting Gregory to school. All of a sudden, *this* became *the* highest priority in my life, in that moment.

I was surrounded by police busily investigating what had happened. Thinking back, the media hadn't noticed I was who I was at that time. It was fortunate. That would come later. I couldn't have imagined what I would have done or said, let alone what I looked like, had they confronted me at that particular moment.

Poor Gregory – he was dressed in sweat pants, and a very dirty tee-shirt, from the night before. He looked pathetic. I looked even more pathetic, still wearing my clothes from the day before. My only thought that I can remember was to clean him up a bit, get some food into him, and get him to his day care at RCC. I needed someone to watch him that I trusted. I needed space, I needed to be alone, and I needed to breathe. After the police gave me the keys to my truck, and a pair of shoes (I was so thankful for something so simple), I took him to Starbucks. I purchased him a lemon bar, two bananas, an apple, and chocolate milk. That was Gregory's breakfast and lunch. I ordered an Americano, with two extra shots of espresso. That was my breakfast and lunch.

The barista looked at me as if I was from another planet. I am not sure if it was because of what I ordered, or because of how Gregory and I looked, or some combination of both. In either case, I obviously looked as if I needed the caffeine, and I did.

I then drove Gregory to the early childhood studies program. I barely remember the quiet drive. After parking, I blindly walked Gregory into the center, as I have not-so-blindly done, hundreds of times. I was surrounded by mothers, fathers, children, faculty and staff. Most I knew personally or at least recognized. Children everywhere – my heart was sinking, and my stomach was churning, with the realization that this was the start of my seeing Garrison's face, in every smiling baby's face, for the rest of my life. I numbly walked Gregory into his classroom, and instantly I felt a big sigh of relief. I don't recall that he was too stressed when I left him. Had he been crying, or reaching out towards me, I think that would have left a huge impression on me. Perhaps he was as comfortable there, as I had hoped?

I spoke to no one. I couldn't even look people in their eyes. I just wanted to get out of there, as quickly as possible. But as I was walking down the hallway to leave, I stopped walking, and began to shake. I was shaking in a manner that I couldn't control. My knees got weak, and I slid my back down the wall until I was sitting on the floor in the main hallway. I just sat there, shaking, but I wasn't crying. I remember turning my head back and forth in a bewildered way, looking to my left and right, hoping not to have been seen by anyone. So far, so good. I struggled to get up, and I knew I had to talk to someone about what happened.

Strange how the body's physiology works, isn't it? In reality, we have little control over most of our bodily functions. Most people don't realize this. Even those of us who do somewhat understand, don't fully realize or appreciate this fact, until it smacks you in the face.

I continued walking down the hallway until I came to the main offices, where I asked for Lynne Vazquez, who is the site supervisor. I asked if she could sit with me for a few minutes. She looked at me with a questioning and caring expression.

This conversation took all of the strength and conviction I could muster. I remember trying to be as "business-like" as I possibly could. I felt weak, and I felt like I couldn't make a rational decision. Even if my life depended on it. This was the first time that I had to use my words to explain what had happened, and to try to express what I would like to be done today, tomorrow, and next week. My God, the look on her face was indescribable. I told her I needed her to be strong. I needed everyone at the ECS program to be strong. I told her that I didn't trust in my judgment, I told her I was so very scared, and knew that I needed Gregory to be watched by many people who had nothing but his best interest at heart. I was so scared that he could react poorly. I was in fear of his over-reacting with shock, anger, or rage. He was so young, and so innocent, and I had no idea what he was going through, or what he would go through.

I felt so sorry for Lynne that morning. I don't know if she realized that she was the first person who I spoke to regarding the murder of Garrison, and what I needed done next. As I left Lynn, I walked into the parking lot, right past people who said hello to me, and I began to cry. I don't know if anyone noticed – I tried hard not to make myself too noticeable.

In hindsight, driving Gregory to RCC's ECS program is when the reality of the situation began to set in. I think it's because no matter how traumatic, how disgusting, how heart-wrenching moments in life are, the Earth continues to rotate, events continue to unfold, and life continues to go on. As I drove, I quickly realized that I needed to get Gregory to RCC to keep his life as "normal" as possible, and as quickly as possible. I needed stability in *his* life. Getting him there became of primary importance. That was my plan for that "today."

At least I knew Gregory would be well taken care of. I didn't know what was in store for me.

Constant tug-of-wars between my intellect and my emotional state: on my intellectual side, I knew that I had to get him to school, and I knew I had to cancel my classes at school. I knew I needed to get help. Emotionally, I was scared to death to ask for help.

I also realized after-the-fact, that my needing to get Gregory safe, would also then allow me to fall apart, emotionally.

Reality Check #2: I Need Help

There I was, standing in the parking lot next to Gregory's classroom. I am not sure if he is sad and crying, or if he was laughing and playing. As I have mentioned previously, he didn't seemed too stressed at the moment that I left. Perhaps he was sleeping, from such an exhausting night. As I try to recall his mood that morning, he was a little quiet, but I remember getting him breakfast and he was in decent spirits. I definitely don't remember any negativity – just quiet sadness.

But now it was about me. He was taken care of, and I had to handle more "situational realities" in my life that morning.

I couldn't fall apart - yet. I wouldn't allow it. I had to continue trying to think straight. I had to cancel my classes. I know I made at least one phone call to school – to the Vice President's office at my college. I remember trying to be very quick, and to the point. I didn't know how to speak about this to anyone else at that time. My bluntness must have come as a shock. I distinctly remember silence on the phone.

Silence on a phone. I can't imagine what it must be like to receive a message like that on the phone. I couldn't imagine hearing that news for the first time.

After calling school, I knew I needed more help, but on a more personal level. Calling the office of my Vice President took care of notifying my friends and colleagues at RCC.

I remember calling my mother. I remember the stunned silence. I remember the emotion of trying to calm her down, but I don't remember specifics or detail on our conversation. I felt that calling my mother took care of notifying my entire family.

But now I needed to make one more phone call, to someone hoping to get the personal help that I so desperately needed. At that moment, there was one person who immediately came to mind, that I knew that I had to call. It was Lori's cousin Steve Jordahl, a man whom I love and respect.

I think I gravitated towards Steve, not only because he was so dear to my heart, but because he was so close to Lori as well. I put my trust in him, on so many different levels. There were a hundred people I could call, and all would have been the right choice. But I was glad that I did call him.

I didn't know what else to do. I knew that I was beginning to fall apart.

He dropped everything in his life that day, and that week. He drove over an hour to me. He spent a few days with me. He drove me everywhere, he took me to the grocery store and helped me shop for food, and he stood beside me and had my back when the media converged on my life. He gave me strength that I didn't feel I had. I reached out for his help, and he delivered. Words are inadequate to express my eternal gratitude to him and his family.

There is so much I don't recall.

I think asking Steve for help was a good choice. I had many family members and friends that would have come in an instant. But honestly, I didn't think I was strong enough to be surrounded by close family. I wanted them near, but I didn't want to have to swim in their emotional presence. Steve gave me someone that I loved, someone I trusted, someone who was also close to Lori and our relationship, but also someone who had enough emotional "distance" from me to give me whatever strength and perspective he could offer.

I also can't overemphasize how instrumental Steve was in helping me during this time. I think bringing in someone you trust as a "coordinator" is one of those pieces of advice that I feel is so vitally important. But, in addition to Steve, I knew I needed more help.

Reality Check #3: Our Physical Health and Well Being

In addition to this whirlwind of activity, I had to think about getting help from differing perspectives. I took Gregory to see his pediatrician on Wednesday, to keep her in the loop, and to ask what to look for physically. I needed to get an idea of what to look for, as signs of shock or stress in a child. What I learned that day, I shared with everyone who would listen. The more eyes on Gregory, the better, as far as I was concerned. From a physical standpoint, Gregory was fine.

I also was acutely aware of the level of stress levels I was under, and to be quite frank, I was concerned for my possibly experiencing a heart attack. I also made an appointment to see our family physician, which Lori and I had seen on multiple occasions. I didn't know him too well, but we did have some history together, and some degree of rapport. We had a frank talk, and he gave me some thoughts of what to look for, from a medical perspective.

He also gave me eight valium tablets, and wanted me to use them. He wanted me to be able to sleep.

Little did I know I wouldn't see him again until the day he testified at the trial. His testimony was of primary focus, regarding Lori's state of mind prior to Garrison's murder.

I found it quite interesting that this physician didn't recognize me at the trial either before or after he testified.

As for me being prescribed valium, I didn't take them. I understood my physician's suggestion of taking them to get good quality sleep. However, I was afraid of falling asleep – Gregory began having bad dreams, and I was afraid of not being able to help him, at a moment's notice.

Sleep deprivation is a primary form of torture, however, and I am sure that my lack of sleep is some evidence of how much I actually tortured myself.

Reality Check #4: Trusting Others

Speaking with the District Attorney's office was the first indication of the legal seriousness of my situation. This happened on Tuesday, the day after Garrison's murder. I met the initial prosecuting deputy D.A., a very nice woman who made me feel very comfortable. Unfortunately, there would be two additional changes in the prosecuting attorney, prior to Lori's murder case going to trial. I guess it was "unfortunate" because, from my perspective, I wished I would have had one person (whoever it was) from beginning to end. That would have given me the "consistency" that I desperately needed. However Will Robinson, the prosecuting attorney at Lori's trial, was wonderful. He made me feel very comfortable.

There were so many things I had to now concentrate on. The trial itself, my dire financial situation, and my impending fights over Gregory were amongst the areas of concern that I now had to pay close attention. The D.A.'s office tried so hard to explain what would be going on, and I didn't hear too much. It was this time that I was first introduced to Kym Conover, who was the director of the Victims Services Unit, of the Riverside County District Attorney's Office. She introduced herself as my primary advocate, and the person who would gently guide me through the entire legal process of the trial, as well as give any assistance that I needed. She was my liaison. She was my confidant. Kym became extremely important in my life. She will always be important in my life. Later I will discuss how she, and her offices, impacted my life.

One of my first concerns was with Gregory's physical well-being, hence our visit to his pediatrician. However this physical concern changed, and I became concerned for his personal safety.

This occurred at Lori's first hearing when she was given a one million dollar bail. My reality shifted dramatically – I knew that there were family members of Lori's who could raise the money to get her out on bail. If this happened, I was very concerned that she would take Gregory.

This fear seemed reasonable to me, yet may have been unjustified to most people. Most would think she would not be released on bail, anyway.

I may have not been thinking rationally on this point, but please forgive me for thinking about extreme circumstances and situations. Whether this was a possibility or not, I acted as if it were. I began to look at life from the perspective as the "worst case" scenario.

I had to.

I made arrangements with the District Attorney's office – if bail were being posted for Lori by someone, as they were filling out the paperwork, I would be notified *during* this paperwork process. I would know that someone was going to get her out of jail, prior to her being released. I would have time to act, accordingly. I made arrangements to "disappear" with Gregory. I know of too many places where I could *not* be found. I was capable of leaving within 30 minutes of that phone call. I had my bags packed, and I just needed to get Gregory and fly or drive away. I knew where my destination was, and I had a very small group of people who would also know where I was, at all times. There was no way that I would let something happen to Gregory.

In addition to working with the D.A.'s office, I had other legal concerns. Would I be put under any scrutiny during the murder trial? Would I need defense counsel? Would I have to fight to keep custody of Gregory? How would I go about getting a divorce? My financial situation was dire, so would I have to consider bankruptcy? What do I do with Garrison's body?

I had so many questions. I needed more help.

One of my first concerns was my immediate monetary situation. I had very little cash, tremendous debt, and absolutely no credit. Within a few days of Garrison's death, I went to my local credit union, and asked to speak with the branch manager. I thought that I would need some credit to help with costs associated with Garrison's death. When I spoke with the branch manager, I asked him for a credit card with a small amount of credit. I explained what had happened, and begged for help. He approved me for a credit card with $2,500 credit. It's funny how such a small thing was so vitally important in my life. He gave that credit to me knowing that I was in financial trouble, in addition to what else was going on in my life. I am very grateful for his help that day.

I was also very aware of Lori and her ability to get what she wants. I feared if she would get out, she would have access to my money from our shared bank accounts, and be able to leave. I also feared that she would intentionally give someone electronic access to the accounts.

My first concern was my monthly pay, so I opened a second account and changed how my pay was direct-deposited.

John Rosario is a man with whom I have worked since I was hired at RCCD. I consider him my mentor and friend. As in most cases, when you work closely with someone, there are times when you don't necessarily see eye-to-eye. There were many times when we conflicted. However, I respect this man so very much, and I listen very carefully to his perspective.

When Garrison was murdered, I was Department Chair of Life Sciences at RCC. John stepped up instantly to assume those duties for my department, as he had been Department Chair previously.

On Wednesday, I traveled to school. Honestly, I don't know why. I guess I felt as if I needed to be busy. But, as soon as I got there, I didn't want to be there. There were so many eyes looking at me and so few words spoken to me. Perhaps they were afraid, perhaps they didn't know.

I remember having a very frank conversation with John, sitting in my office, with the door shut, for about an hour. He asked quite a few very blunt questions, and listened very carefully. He gave me a gut check on many topics. As I have mentioned, I was fearful of having a heart attack. I was fearful of succumbing to stress, and because of this, I was very fearful of Gregory's future. The reality is that if I did die, Lori would get all of my life insurance, as well as my retirement benefits, because we were still married.

John and I discussed my getting additional life insurance, and what my wishes were if I were to die. I made the decision to make John the executer of Gregory's estate. I needed him to be strong, I needed him to make rational decisions for Gregory's best interest, and I needed him to work closely with those who would be charged with raising Gregory, in the event of my death.

Later that week, I had no choice but to get an independent life insurance policy, which had nothing to do with Lori. This hurt – I didn't have much money. I made John the beneficiary, if in the event I died. I knew he would make sure Gregory would finish his education, and he would give Gregory the best start possible, to the rest of his life. The policy I got was more than enough for Gregory for a very, very, long time.

This was all an important reality check for me. Allowing myself to place my full trust in others, and letting them help me, was crucial.

I can't overemphasize how important this was.

I had other legal issues to deal with. Now I had to concern myself with family and financial legal matters. I asked another one of my life-long friends of mine for legal help. Lisa Patterson and I met in graduate school. I adore her and her family very much. They have welcomed me into their lives as if I was their own. They also have a long and rich legal history (spanning over 60 years). I knew her family was very well respected legally, and I knew that Lisa would be that strong voice which would rationally guide me through any legal issues that might arise. Lisa immediately arranged to have criminal legal counsel for me available, should any need arise prior to or during the trial. She also arranged for me to meet with a top bankruptcy attorney, and attended our meetings along with me and Steve. She also arranged for me to meet with a divorce attorney.

Lisa took care of all of this for me. I couldn't imagine dealing with those aspects of my life without her.

My first personal appearance in court was a hearing in family court the following week, in front of a judge, to ask for sole custody of Gregory, to request no visitation rights for Lori, and to get permission to leave the state, if I chose to travel.

As I first stood in that courtroom, there were literally dozens of people, having each of their own conversations. It was a very "busy" place. But, when I explained the rationale behind my requests, you could hear a pin drop in the courtroom.

The judge granted me my wishes that day.

Reality Check #5: Institutional Ambivalence

My loss is not alone.

June 4, 1983. An 11-year old teenager asking for permission to spend the night at his friend's home, and receiving permission, from his loving parents.

June 5, 1983. The loving father, driving back to the house, planning on picking up his son.

He didn't deserve to find what he found.

Bill Hughes was the director of the Arabian Horse Unit, and Professor of Animal Science, at the California State Polytechnic University, in Pomona, California. I was an undergraduate student at Cal Poly at the time, and I knew him casually, and I had taken one course with him. I can't say that I knew him extremely well, though.

That morning, Bill Hughes walked into the Ryan household, expecting to find a loving family and his son.

What Bill Hughes found must have shaken his sense of reality. He found the bodies of Douglas and Peggy Ryan, their daughter Jessica, and his son Christopher. He also found his son's friend, Josh, but just barely alive. The bodies had been cut, and they had been mutilated. According to testimony, they were brutally attacked, chopped with a hatchet, sliced with a knife, and stabbed multiple times with an ice pick.

As a student at Cal Poly during these murders, I distinctly remember the shock the entire community had experienced. The shock of the actual event, and the drawn-out search for the possible murderer was in the news every day. The eventual capture of the prime suspect, Kevin Cooper, the trial, his conviction and eventual sentence to death was very much in the public spotlight.

This has continued to cause public controversy. Kevin Cooper's conviction is seen by some as a travesty of justice, and it is still at the center of the "death penalty" debate here in California. The extensive media coverage has made this a very important part of the local history in southern California.

That was the public aspect of this case.

In no way would I ever assume what they privately went through, nor would I ever suggest what I think they may have experienced. My personal experience and Bill Hughes' do have some similarity, but in my humble opinion only superficially. I now have a better idea of what happened to him, of how he tried (from my narrow perspective) to rebuild his life, and most especially, how he tried to rebuild his career.

This is an important segue into my next topic – how Cal Poly Pomona treated Bill Hughes, at least from my perspective of a student at the University at that time. Bill Hughes was not seen on campus for a very long time. This was completely understandable, and quite honestly, expected. It seemed to me as if he took quite a lot of time off from school in order to deal with the logistics of this case, and for his family to heal. Time was of the essence for him. Again, I am not aware of the specifics of how Cal Poly helped Bill Hughes, but from the "outside" it seemed as if the University did what it could to support Bill Hughes and his family.

This was not the case for me.

Riverside Community College District has policies in place to support District personnel with personal sickness or tragedy. There are many polices available, and many different options, depending on the situation. However, many of these policies aren't written and are subject to personal interpretations.

In my case, RCCD, as an institution, was not supportive of me. There were *individuals* who were incredibly supportive, and for whom I am eternally grateful, but as an *institution* there was very little support. I cannot say that there was absolutely no support, but very little. Let me illustrate.

My wife murdered my 17 month old son. This heinous act, the murder of my son Garrison at the hands of his own mother, was not deemed "catastrophic" by my District.

As explained to me, had I been diagnosed with cancer, had Lori or one of my sons been diagnosed, or had Lori died in a car wreck – those would have been deemed "catastrophic" by the District. Had this catastrophic designation taken place, I could have taken off as much time from work as I needed for me and my family. As it was, I was forced to come back to work much earlier than I should have.

I very rarely take time off of work (as many of my disgruntled students would attest), and as part of my contract I get "sick" or "personal" days every year. If I don't use them, they accrue through time. In actuality, this forms a "bank account" of unused days. I have, on occasion, donated my accrued days to another District employee when they needed additional time for their catastrophic issues.

I always thought of this as a kind act, a small token of my heart, and one in which I could help them overcome their tragedy.

If memory serves me correct, when Garrison died I had somewhere around 70 unused sick/personal days accrued. Obviously, the day of the murder, and every day afterwards, I cashed in (or used) my personal days. I was under the assumption that there would be days donated to me for later use.

However, the District made the determination that my situation wasn't "catastrophic". Because it wasn't deemed "catastrophic", no faculty or staff in the District was allowed to donate their sick/personal days towards my "bank" of accrued time.

My accrued 70 (or so) time, had I "cashed" it all in, would have been equivalent to taking about a semester off. I could have done that but it would have left me with no additional days in the bank for the impending trial. I knew I would have to take time off for that. I also knew I needed time to heal.

I will never forget the meeting, when I was informed of the decision to not deem the murder of my son at the hands of his mother "catastrophic". I was not informed of this decision by the person who made the decision. This news was extremely devastating to me; it was in opposition to what I had been led to believe would probably happen. I literally had dozens of colleagues (that I knew of), each of whom were willing to donate me dozens of days. This would have given me the necessary time to recover from my wife murdering my son.

I just lost my son at the hands of his mother. I just lost my wife...

My District, the institution itself, deemed this "not catastrophic." Dealing with the loss, my life ripped apart at its core, and facing a new life and its new reality – was deemed "not catastrophic."

I wasn't given the time that I desperately needed to heal. This wasn't even an option. I also wasn't given the time I would need to deal with the impending trial.

And to think, that this decision was strictly up to an individual's personal *interpretation* of my contract of employment. A conversation, by the way, I was not a part of.

No one, at any time, asked me what I would like.

Not my Union. Not my administrators. Not my colleagues.

No one, especially those who may have been involved with this decision, has ever explained to me the rationale behind this decision.

Every day that I took off, removed a day from my account. Even days I didn't have classes were counted against my account (that semester I didn't have scheduled classes on Fridays, but every Friday was removed from the account as well). This is a very convenient way of the District saving a tremendous amount of money.

Garrison's murder happened in the third week of the semester. I was taking time off for grieving.

However, the realization that the impending trial would also take a lot of my time hit me like a ton of bricks.

Had I been a juror on a major trial, I would have been paid to sit on the jury, and I would have been able to take time off from teaching, as part of my legal obligations as a juror.

However, I was a "witness" in a major murder trial, and therefore I couldn't be compensated or take time off.

From my perspective, I just couldn't get a break.

Imagine being told that the murder of your son wasn't "catastrophic" enough to warrant taking more time off, not "catastrophic" enough to allow colleagues to donate their accrued time to help me heal. Imagine my dismay when I learned that this was a single persons "interpretation" of the contract, and that person's opinion couldn't be discussed, or appealed, once it was made.

I realized that I would not have enough accrued time to be able to withstand the requirements of my personal grief, and in addition the required time that the trial would consume. From an intellectual perspective, the trial had to take immediate priority in my life, and screw my emotional healing.

Therefore I had no choice but to go back to work. I had to stand in front of students, and teach collegiate biology.

I had to stand in front of students, who were immediately impacted by Garrison's death. They all knew what had happened, and each and every one of them had their own unique grieving experience.

I had to be professional in the classroom. I had to attend meetings. I had to do all of this, in less than 40 days of Garrison's murder.

Missing The Links

I cannot say that my District did not support me, in any manner. When I did come back, I didn't have to teach every one of my classes. The District did make the decision to bring in a substitute professor, to teach some of these courses. This lessened my load when I came back, and I am very grateful for this. In essence, I came back part-time, versus full time. I am very appreciative of this fact. However, the fact that I was required to come back, at all, so soon really hurt me, emotionally. This unilateral decision by the District was a tough one for me to accept.

Don't get me wrong…

Had I joined my family in its business, and not attended University, I would have been operating bulldozers and doing construction. Many people who have suffered tragic loss don't have the opportunities that I have in my life, and most would not be able to take *any* time off. I am very humbled by this reality, one by which I have worked hard to attain. However, I was told that it would all work out, and then was informed of the decision that my situation wasn't "catastrophic" enough – and that hurt very hard.

I should have never gone back in front of the classroom that quickly. I was not a valuable member of the faculty, and did not give my District their "monies worth" that they required of me. I couldn't think straight, and it was very obvious.

I am so thankful for my compassionate colleagues and friends at RCC. I am also so incredibly thankful for my students who had to see me walk through that door every day for the rest of that semester. They were wonderful.

People were wonderful. *They* weren't ambivalent.

It was.

The institution, that is.

My Focus: Our Psychological Health and Well Being

My situational reality morphed at some point. I went from having to make decision after decision, which added stress and exhaustion to my already stressed and exhausted mind and body, to a more consistent daily dullness in my life.

I went from dealing with situation after situation, to dealing with consistent issues or themes. I guess it went from living in each moment, to realizing that I needed to also deal with issues from a larger perspective.

Gregory began having bad dreams, almost instantly. I am so very fortunate that he openly spoke to me about the dreams, and I am lucky that I had typed lots of notes in my journal. The final interpretations can be up to professionals (or to you the reader), but here is basically what happened in Gregory's nighttime hours, for the next few weeks after he lost his little brother.

On Wednesday, two days after Garrison died, Gregory told me that he had a dream about Garrison standing in the entry of the house, in front of the front door to the house. He was surrounded by many toys on the ground. Garrison was standing there, kicking at the toys, apparently frustrated. Gregory asked if he was ok, and Garrison looked at him, smiled, and said yes.

On Thursday, Gregory had another vivid dream. This time Gregory and I were standing in our backyard of the same house, and Garrison was trying to open the side gate to get out of the backyard. He was again flustered. Evidently, I kept shutting the gate on him, keeping him from going outside, which added to his frustration.

On Friday morning, after telling me about this dream, Gregory took me to see some pictures of Garrison hanging on a bedroom wall, and pointed to one of the pictures of Garrison sleeping. When he did this, I was concerned that the pictures may be causing him stress. I asked him if he wanted to keep the pictures of Garrison on his wall, and he said yes. He wanted to see Garrison's face.

We ended up having a very a nice talk, and Gregory sat in my lap facing me, and we embraced each other. I don't ever remember being as close to another human, as we were sitting in the sunlight on this morning. I cried – hard. It was one of the first times I cried when someone else was around. I told Gregory that we needed to always remember Garrison, and that it was ok to dream about him. He could always play and talk with him in his dreams. This was so incredibly tough for me, but I feel that it was so incredibly good for Gregory.

On Friday night, Gregory said that he had another dream. This time he and Garrison were sitting in the living room, and playing with toys together. It seemed as if it was a very pleasant dream. Gregory said he liked playing with Garrison, even in his dreams.

Wednesday, March 11. Gregory had another dream about Garrison. They were at the early childhood studies center together, and Garrison was dressed up as "Elmo" and playing outside. Gregory asked him how he was doing, and Garrison looked at him, smiled, and said he was OK.

Everything would be ok.

There were more, but I felt that the initial dreams that Gregory shared with me are insightful. They were filled with frustration, with joy, to Garrison being blocked by barriers. Yet all had an overall theme that everything would be alright.

I was most happy that Gregory was telling me about his dreams, and was continuing to open up.

My Strategy with Gregory

I am not sure exactly how to interpret the dreams that Gregory was having, but as I said I was happy that Gregory was in fact dreaming, and even more so that he was talking about them. I didn't care if he talked to me about them, but I really wanted him to talk to *someone* about them.

Every day I took Gregory to the Early Childhood Center (ECS). Every day I picked him up. No matter if I felt good when I woke up, no matter if I felt as if I wanted to bury myself into a cocoon, I would make sure that Gregory went to the Center. Gregory needed normalcy, he needed consistent routine, and he needed a place to find solace and peace.

At the center, Lynne Vazquez was incredibly instrumental in Gregory's welfare. She did a tremendous amount of coordination and training with her staff, much of which I am aware, and a lot of which I remain unaware. Lynne brought in psychological experts who specialized in post-traumatic stress in infants, in order to brief the staff on what signs of stress to look for. Not only signs of stress in Gregory, but with the other children at the center as well.

This was all so traumatic for everyone – the children, their families, the staff (and their families).

Lynne also worked with other families who had their children with Gregory at the Center. She is the person who had to inform all of the families about Garrison's death. She wrote a letter, as a formal document, which officially informed everyone what had happened. She realized that this was a trauma suffered by everyone there, and it was indeed a "team effort" that was needed.

I treated every day as a "de-brief" when I dropped off Gregory, and also when I picked him up. I was very blunt and up-front with any potential signs of trauma or stress that Gregory showed, and I fully expected everyone at the Childcare Center (ECS) to be watching Gregory, for all that was good and bad, and to be vigilant for outward signs of stress. I shared with them all that was good and bad about Gregory's habits at home as well. I must have been annoying at times, and seeing me come and go must have caused consternation. I hope it wasn't as bad as I imagined.

As I have stated many times, I felt ignorant in what signs to look for in Gregory, and I relied upon others more qualified than I to work with me in Gregory's best interest. At times I didn't trust my judgment.

It was a team effort that I wanted, and it was a team effort that helped Gregory through his trauma so splendidly.

I have never sat down to think about it, but sitting here, at this moment, I think I can summarize how I tried to raise Gregory at this time in several ways. I surrounded myself with people with his best interest at heart, and I guess I followed a few guiding principles for how I either communicated or parented Gregory. I didn't do this intentionally, but I did come to realize that these were "themes" that Gregory and I consistently had conversations about, and I think that these themes were a driving force for me and Gregory over the next few months.

- Nothing that happened was his fault.

- He is valued and loved.

- It's ok to for us to cry.

- It's ok to be mad, even at me.

- What he thinks is important, and I want to hear about it.

- I must be consistent with my standards for him, and in his discipline.

- It's ok to trust someone.

I think one of my main fears when his brother was murdered by his mother was his loss of faith in people, especially in women. When I think about the drastic changes in Gregory's life that occurred in a blink on of an eye – the loss his little brother and his best friend by the hand of his mother, the actual loss of his mother (his other best friend), and the essential loss his older step-brother – his sense of reality must have been shaken to the core. *Everything* he held dear had either betrayed him, or abandoned him. *Everything* that he trusted, cherished, and loved, was gone.

Everything that is, except for me, and those surrounding him who truly care...

How could he ever trust a woman again? How could he ever build a future and a family, when his foundation was destroyed?

Missing The Links

I want Gregory to grow up as a "normal" child. I want him to have strength, conviction, a strong work ethic, principles, morals, a good sense of humor, and an optimistic outlook. I want him to be sincere, and be able to place trust in his relationships and friendships.

Obviously, this is what any of us would want in our child. Add to the normal stresses of childhood and growing up the trauma and realization that this murder inflicted.

Getting Gregory counseling was of primary importance to me. Within a few days of the murder, I asked Kym Conover at Victim Services if there was a list or group of counselors who dealt with children traumatic therapy. She kindly provided a short list.

I began calling and speaking with every individual on that list, or at least the ones that would speak with me. Sadly, I didn't feel comfortable with any single one. Not one said "let me help." A few were ambivalent, a few seemed to be overwhelmed by the situation, and as I alluded, a few didn't respond to my multiple attempts to contact them.

So I asked Kym for additional names…

The first name on this second list answered the phone. She said that she was very much aware of the case, and would love to help Gregory. That was all I needed. We decided to meet, and this allowed her to get to know both me and Gregory.

In the interest of Gregory's privacy, and in the interest of confidentiality, I will not mention this therapist's name. However, the importance of this person in my life cannot be overemphasized, and I am so very grateful. I will remain so, until the day that I die.

Play therapy.

What a wonderful concept. Of course, I had heard about it, as most people have. But watching Gregory and his therapist undergo this type of communication was a wonderful (as well as painful) experience.

The basic idea is to allow a child the opportunity to get into a "comfort zone" while his focus is on play. Using a child's imagination, and allowing the child to express his emotions through play such as using building blocks to build cities, expressing anger through destroying those cities, drawing pictures with his joy and to express his joy, his anger, his fears, his sadness. Playing with dolls, being nice to dolls, torturing dolls – there are so many aspects of how insightful play therapy is.

Through my experiences, I came to the realization and understanding that the thought processes of a child are far more complicated than most people would realize, or are capable of admitting. I came to realize that their inability to express their emotions and thoughts is primarily limited to their lack of verbal language and skill. Allowing them to play is a form of communication, getting a child comfortable, and allowing them to express themselves. Now when I see children get upset, I can easily imagine them knowing what is happening in their minds, but being driven "nuts" by the inability of *us adults* to understand what *they* are trying to say. This is often a good source of infuriation with adults, as well.

There were aspects of Gregory's therapy that I would expect. Trying to get Gregory to express his sadness, how much he misses his mother and brother, and to share his frustrations with me were very important.

One thing that I didn't initially expect is when he began expressing his absolute anger with his mother.

Gregory was so young. He was only 39 months old when Garrison's murder happened. Yet for being so young, he was incredibly insightful, and it took some work, but he eventually was able to express what he was thinking and why.

A three and a half year old child, using his words, articulately, verbally expressing his anger. I am so proud of him. Most adults are incapable of doing this.

Gregory never struggled with, or fought against his therapy. He never tried to avoid the issue. Even when introduced to a stranger (like with his therapist), he would answer questions relatively easily and openly. He seemed as if he was comfortable with who he was, from the beginning.

It was just over three weeks after Garrison had died, and I was sitting with Gregory as he was taking a bath. I sat with him quite often during bath time. Sometimes I would just lie back on the floor, sometimes sitting up against the wall. This was quality time with my son. Sometimes we would talk. Sometimes we would cry. Sometimes we would play. Sometimes I wouldn't do a thing – just be with Gregory.

"Where's Mommy?"

One of the most basic questions a child asks. How simple, how succinct, and how loving. A mother's love, a mother's trust, and a mother's nurturing nature. With mommy not there, life must indeed be different for a young child. How often he must ask himself that question. How much does he really want an answer? How could I answer this basic question, if he ever asked?

The funny thing is that I suddenly noticed that Gregory had *never* asked this important question. I realized that he had never asked *for* his mother. When I realized this, I was startled, and dismayed.

Weeks had gone by since Garrison's murder. Gregory never, not once, asked *for* his mommy. He never asked when she was coming home or when he would get to see her. Initially, he never said that he missed her. His expressing his missing her came about two years later, during the murder trial. But during this initial time of turmoil, I suddenly noticed that he hadn't asked *for* her, and this was quite a reality check with me.

My words are undoubtedly not describing what was happening with Gregory in full context, so please be patient, and forgive me.

He did ask *about* his mother, but he never asked *for* her.

I have always thought this was important – why didn't he ever ask *for* his mother? I would have assumed that at some point, he would want to see his mother, and he would want a hug from her. Something. That, to me, seems reasonable.

Perhaps this little man understood more than most might give him credit for…

When he did ask *about* his mother, his questions were very specific.

"*Where's mommy?*"

"She is with the police at the police station" I said.

"*Is mommy ok?*"

"Yes, the police are taking care of her, and she is alright."

"Why did mommy kill my baby Garrison?"

My heart stopped.

"Honey, I don't know. I wish I could explain." That is all I could muster, fighting back my own tears.

He asked so many questions, which would then inspire so many conversations, and then more questions. Sometimes Gregory would pose these questions at home, and other times he would pose questions during the oddest places or times. We could be driving in the car, or shopping at the grocery store, for instance.

Many of these questions I simply couldn't answer.

When this happened, I made sure that I would freely admit if I didn't know something, and that if I ever found out, I would let Gregory know. In other times, he would ask questions that I felt the answer would not be appropriate for him. My range of responses went from gently guiding him away from the subject, to stating very matter-of-fact (like) "I won't talk to you about that right now. I promise that someday we will talk about that." I was blunt, but in a nurturing way. Gregory always, I think, appreciated that. He never, ever, fought me for more information.

How would you suggest answering a question like "how did mommy hurt Garrison?" to a three year old?

People have given me a wide range of suggestions and responses, when they inquire about how I have treated Gregory. From support, to questioning how I use my language with him. That's ok. Gregory knows that any question he asks is alright to ask.

There are no bad questions. He knows that I will give him my time, and he also knows that there are some things that he doesn't need to know about – at least yet.

I always took my time to stop what we were doing, either kneel or sit down and look at him eye-to-eye, and I always asked him what he was feeling. I think this is one of the most important things I could have done and so I still continue to do. Give him my undivided attention, in that moment. I can't imagine how many times, while we were driving, I would just pull over and talk with him for a while.

I just felt that if a moment hit him, *we had to live that moment* - together. Pushing it off, as most people would easily do, would minimize its importance, and I want Gregory to know that he is important, and what he has to say is important.

I also knew that our speaking was also in my best interest, and an important part of my personal therapy. I also knew that I was nurturing and fostering life-long trust with my son.

I tried very hard to watch what I said, and how I said it. I didn't want my emotional pain, my anger, or my confusion to add to his weight. However, I did want him to share in my pain, and my sadness, in a way that was in Gregory's best interest.

It's ok for Gregory to see me hurting. It's ok for Gregory to see me in pain. What Gregory also needed to see is how I dealt with it...

This was all so hard on me, needless to say.

"Why did mommy kill my baby Garrison?"

How would a three year old come up with that question?

I suddenly realized that this must have been my fault.

I believe he heard me say something, to that effect, when I was on the phone, driving in the car. I was angry, and I was venting. However, he heard it. I wasn't careful enough, and his simple question rocked my world. I knew that I had to be more careful, I had to be more considerate and passionate to Gregory and what he was thinking, and I had to think hard at each and every moment. Those moments would help shape Gregory's life.

Again, I had to focus.

My Stepson

In suffering our loss, I had a certain measure of control over what help both Gregory and I received. No matter how hard it was, it was just simply the right thing to do. My stepson Nicholas, on the other hand, was a different matter. Other than Garrison himself, I believe that Nick suffered in this tragedy more than anyone else. His mother was an incredibly important part of his life, and his experience may have scarred him forever.

This is a difficult thing for me to discuss. I have spent so much time on this section, having written and re-written it, on formulating and re-formulating my thoughts, and exactly how I want to say what I am feeling deep inside. I have concluded that there are a few basic areas where I am the most concerned, and how Nick, Gregory, and I have grown together – to a limited extent.

- What happened in the days prior to, and including, Garrison's murder.

- How has the loss of Lori in Nick's life impacted him?

- How has Nick reacted since the murder occurred?

Since the day of the murder, my personal role in Nick's life has changed drastically. Not that I have a romantic vision of my role as a "father figure" in Nick's life, but I do feel that Nick and I have a pretty good relationship. I was the outsider. I was the step-dad. I knew my place, and I was humble enough to both realize and accept this fact. But, I do think that I brought Nick a lot of good examples as a role model. My easy going demeanor, my strong work ethic, and my genuine interest in him are something that was easy for me to convey. I love Nick. He is a good kid, and he has a chance to become an amazing man. My seeing him as an older brother, with Gregory, and then with Garrison, melted my heart. He has always had so much pure love for his brothers. But, Nick had his two parents, and I was on the periphery, and I knew it.

Whatever "good" I brought to Nick was also removed, to a major extent, the day of the murder. When Nick's father picked him up from the police station, Nick was, in essence, removed from my care, and from my influence.

I cannot begin to imagine, or comprehend, what happened to Nick during the days surrounding the murder. My heart bleeds for Nick, and what he went through. The journey that Nick took with his mother during this time is, as it should be, the subject of a book in and of itself. Nick's insight of what his experience was would be of incredible value. Imagine a teenager's prism, watching his mother slowly slip down a slope of despair, which culminates in the murder of his little brother.

Unfortunately, Nick wasn't just a bystander. By keeping Nick home on that fateful day, Lori included Nick in a very disgustingly intimate manner. Nick saw her at her worst, and Nick saw the last remnants of his mother fly away into the abyss. Nick was indeed innocent in Garrison's murder, and is not to blame for any aspect of what his mother did. But, for reasons only known to her, Lori decided to "include" Nick on the final destination in her sickening journey. For the life of me, I can't wrap my head around that fact.

I have previously illustrated the amount of time that Lori and Nick spent together in the days prior to the murder. Nick has shared some of these experiences with me personally, as well as having to share these during testimony and under oath in the trial. Nick saw the rapid decline in his mother. Nick was privy to Lori's thoughts during this time, experienced her reality from an intimate perspective, and in my opinion was tortured psychologically. Not only did he know what his mother had done, he had been witness to his little brother's body. Nick found Garrison's body earlier in the day, prior to my coming home. He had seen his mother acting in a psychotic state.

He was more intimately aware of what Lori was experiencing than I was, because of this valuable time he spent with her over the weekend and on that fateful morning.

She kept him home that day – the day of the murder. I do not know why she made that decision, but that decision may have scarred him forever.

Nick sat in that house the entire day...

Nick had found Garrison's body...

Nick saw and heard a woman who was once his mother...

Nick saw me come home with Gregory. Nick sat there as I prepared dinner. Nick didn't know what to do, or what to say...

Nick told me that his mother didn't want to be disturbed...

Nick agreed with my suggestion that I leave for a while…

Nick saw me leave the house, and Nick sat there with his younger brother Gregory, at his side, on that couch…

Nick knew that if his mother came out again, while I was gone, that *he* would have to battle *her* to protect his little brother…

I discovered much later that Nick, sitting on that couch all alone, fearing that his mother could come out again, sat with a knife at his side…

Fearing that he would have to fight his mother…

Fearing that more would happen…

Not knowing what to do…

And he was alone…

Hopelessly alone…

Again.

My heart bleeds for Nick.

He got to play with his little brother that morning. He got to see the last smiles of Garrison's life. He got to hear the last laughter in Garrison's life. Nick witnessed his mother's actions the hours prior to Garrison's murder. Nick evidently heard the sound when his mother hit Garrison over the head. Nick heard the silence afterwards. Nick saw his mother in a psychotic state. Lori telling Nick that "everything would be ok." Nick hearing Lori say, over and over, "trust me."

So much detail that I have intentionally left out. So much detail that I am unaware of…

"Everything will be ok."

"Trust me."

These are the most harmful, intentionally hurtful and scarring words that Lori could have ever said to Nick. I fear he is scarred from these words for the rest of his life. How could he ever trust a woman again?

I tell many stupid jokes in my lecture classes, generally intended to sarcastically make a point. One joke when discussing Mendelian genetics says "the two worst words a guy can say to a woman is 'trust me.' The two worst words a woman says to a man is 'it's yours!'"

I usually get quite a bit of laughter, and quite a few heads shaking, but always with a smile.

A joke has context. A joke has focus, and meaning. A joke is meant to make you laugh, to relax you, and sometimes look at the most basic aspect of human existence, from the perspective of humor. Good humor tends to make you look closely at yourself.

"Trust me."

It hurts me to even think about these words spoken to Nick during those days.

As you may have gathered, Lori is strong-willed. In a co-parenting relationship, she was often domineering, over-powering, and was the primary disciplinarian. This is true for Lori's parenting Nick – when compared to his father. I knew this was the case, having seen this on many occasions. However, as a husband and co-parent with her for over three years, I also saw a woman who had standards, and worked hard to maintain those standards.

Lori and I clashed on how to achieve those standards, but we agreed on what the standards were, or so I had thought.

Once Lori was arrested, her absence left a vacuum in Nick's life, both in a good and bad way. My focus here is on her impact and the vacuum of her absence, both good and bad, on Nick's growth and development.

Lori's loss as a daily part of our lives began to expose "cracks" in their relationship, which already existed. Instantly, Lori was removed as a parent in Nick's life. Take this statement for what it is. Like most things in life, there is no 100% good, or 100% bad. She was gone. With that absence, the good was removed, along with the bad.

Nick and Lori had a close relationship, albeit a rocky one. Nick was what would be considered a normal teenager, with the normal amount of angst, anger, and self-esteem issues that most teenagers have. Since the first day I met Nick, he has also been angry. My guess is that his anger comes from his predispositions to anger, his reacting to his parents splitting up, or any other of a host of reasons. This anger often caused tension between him and his parents, and on occasion between me and him. But, in my opinion, this tension between us was to be expected, and it wasn't anything I was ever too overly concerned with. I am convinced that my patience was the key with me and Nick. My perspective of Nick's relationships with his parents is viewed from my prism of reality, just as my impressions of his relationship with me. Many of my opinions, I am quite sure, could be questioned – however, I humbly feel that what I say comes from a good place.

The night of the murder, I saw a wide range of emotional responses from Nick. Not only was he extremely angry over what Lori had done, but I distinctly remember Nick *begging me* not to hurt his mother, and his expressing despair at the realization that she would be arrested. He did not want his mother taken away.

He was torn between his protective mechanisms for this woman who was so important in his life, and his anger and pain from what she did.

In my opinion, he knew that as she was taken away by the police, she was being taken away from his life, as well.

Like I have said many, many times, my main hope is that Nick becomes a good 25-year old, because his journey into young adulthood was so traumatic and problematic. The chances of the "good" 25 year-old "target" for a time seemed to have little chance to be achieved.

I originally was going to call this entire section "sex, drugs, and rock-n-roll." These few words, to an extent, would be an adequate description of how Nick dealt with this tragedy.

Nick needed help, desperately. He needed professional help. I was smart enough to know that that both Gregory and I needed help. It wasn't an intellectual leap to also see that Nick needed help, most desperately.

Quite simply, Nick didn't feel he needed help, and quite bluntly, his father didn't make him get any help. I have many examples to illustrate this, but suffice it to say I arranged for Nick to get counseling three times, and I arranged to have his counseling paid for completely, with any counselor of his choice. Nick didn't like any counselor he met. Excuse after excuse. Nick and his father lost any financial opportunity that I had arranged, so that they could get the help that he needed. This was especially true, at the beginning of his tragic journey, when Nick needed it the most. Nick felt that he could just talk with his friends, and work out his own problems, on his own terms.

Nick fought adamantly against being forced to get help. His dad succumbed to these wishes, and I was powerless. I was an outsider – I wasn't his father, so legally I couldn't force Nick to get help. All I could do is peer into his life from the outside, and hope for the best. I couldn't do anything serious about it. As I will illustrate at the end of this chapter, this became a major focus of my victim's impact statement to the court.

Not only did Nick refuse to get help, his life took a predicted downward spiral of an angry teenager with no guidance or supervision. He partied hard, got in trouble with his school and the law, and went through multiple relationships with women. I choose not to illustrate many of these examples, out of respect for who Nick is, and my sincere hope that he continues his growth into a good man.

I also feel that deep down inside, Nick has always known what was right, and what was wrong. He has also known what he should have been doing. He needed to get help. He needed to vent his frustrations toward both his mother and father. He needed to resist the urge to bury his pain chemically. This is one of the reasons why he decided to move out-of-state to live with extended family. He could begin a "new life" and get away from his father, from me, from Gregory, and everything that kept reminding him of what happened. He told me once that he couldn't bear looking into Gregory's eyes, because of the pain that it brought.

But before he made this decision to move, I remember a conversation we had on the phone, where he told me how desperate he was, and how sad he was. He asked if he could move in with me and Gregory. I told him, at any time, he was welcomed to move in with us. But, with a few conditions, which weren't negotiable. He had to stay in school and give it the best effort he could, he had to spend a lot time with Gregory, and most importantly, he had to go to therapy twice a week for six months. After that, depending on how he was doing, we would re-assess his situation.

He chose not to move in with Gregory and me. My terms weren't acceptable.

He chose to move out-of-state, and away from everything.

Prior to his move, I also tried hard to convince him to stay here. As I explained to him, moving would have many good aspects for him. However, it was my sincere opinion that by his "running away" to start a new life, and his not honestly facing his issues, his troubles would not simply "go away". His troubles, as I honestly thought, would simply follow him wherever he went. I tried to convince him to keep working on school here, to get serious counseling, and to make his life here. Then, after a few years, he could move anywhere he wanted, and he could become anything he wanted. I also knew if he left, the quality time he could spend with Gregory would diminish radically, or disappear entirely. However, the reality was that he wasn't spending any quality time with Gregory anyway, so from an un-emotional perspective, that wouldn't have been a great loss.

He did move, and he was welcomed with open arms by loving family. But, as I feared, his troubles followed. There were more of the same personal problems, angst, and anger. In addition, his father followed Nick to the same city and neighborhood. Suddenly, he was in trouble, all over again. For all of his rationale, and for all of his reasoning, his troubles did as I feared they would – they followed him with his move.

I could still do nothing to help him.

I still can't, other than being optimistic, and being there for him as well as encouraging him to spend as much quality time as possible with Gregory. However, I do have rules and standards for Gregory, and I hold Nick to those same standards.

I love Nick dearly, and I will do anything I can to help him become that good 25 year old man.

My Strategy with Myself

I also reached out for professional help, for myself.

My initial concerns during my therapy, were to give me coping skills to make my daily life bearable. How to wake up, how to get Gregory ready for school, and how to keep my life taped together in a reasonable fashion.

With time, my therapy evolved into how to deal with my anger towards what Lori had done, my resentment over how I felt manipulated by her prior to the murder, my pity for her, and my protectiveness over all that I held dear.

I am still trying to answer these basic questions. I suppose that I will continue to do this, for the rest of my life.

I was miserable. Having my life ripped apart, my impending financial doom, and still living in the rental house where Garrison had died began to take a toll.

My first reaction was to get the hell out of that house. But I didn't think I could, or even that I should. First of all, I didn't think I had even a slim chance to save my home, the one that Lori and I had vacated when we chose to rent instead. But more importantly, I felt that if I moved, it would add to Gregory's stress levels, bringing too much change in Gregory's life too soon. Losing his little brother, losing his mother, and being forced to move once again were too much in my opinion. I honestly felt that if I immediately moved Gregory into a new place that it would add too much turmoil to his life.

The actual night of the murder, I was very careful to shield Gregory from any visual trauma – he hadn't seen Garrison's body, and he didn't see any of the blood. He heard the energy of the moments surrounding the arrests, and he saw his mother being led away, but I felt that he didn't have any "scarring" visual memories of the murder, so living in that house added needed stability to his life.

Those images are burned into my memory, not his.

Perhaps I was wrong. Perhaps I should have moved immediately. But Gregory never, not once, showed any signs of stress. I believe that I was more stressed than he was, living in that house.

Should I stay, or should I go?

I made the decision to stay in that house, for Gregory's sake. Now I was living in the house where Garrison had been murdered. I was looking at the bathroom where I found Lori naked in the cold shower staring at me with those soulless eyes. I was seeing the hallways and bedroom where Garrison's murder took place.

That rental never felt like it was my "home" anyway. My home, the house that we had purchased, was vacated, and empty. It was difficult, but I managed to stay there in the rental house for about two additional months following the murder.

I noticed that my stress levels were consistently rising. My emotions were morphing from terrible sadness and loss, to worrying about my immediate and long-term future. I became more and more uncomfortable with staying in the rental house where Garrison had died, even though Gregory seemed to be doing quite well.

I gathered the strength to make a few phone calls to inquire about my home. I learned that if there were any chance at all to save my home, I absolutely had to live in it.

This realization made my decision easier, so I decided to move from the rental house, back into my home.

So, again, I asked for help. I let everyone know what was happening, and that I needed to move back to my home.

Saturday, May 9th, 2009. Two and a half months after Garrison's death. A virtual army showed up to help me move. It was an amazing display of frantic activity, but all of it was worthwhile. My family and friends helped me and Gregory move back into my home in one day. What an emotionally exhausting day. I don't think I did a damn thing. Moving out of the house where Garrison died was monumental in my life – a move towards my independence, a move away from Lori, and a first step towards my new life with Gregory.

My Focus: Being strong for my family, friends, and colleagues.

My world has changed, and how I look at the world has changed. I look at myself differently. I look at others very differently. I have noticed that my patience and empathy for those who are indeed sincere is limitless. I have also noticed that my patience for those who are manipulative, conniving, and self-serving is minute. I experience this every day in my personal life, as well as in my professional life.

I have so many examples of my feeling so alone, so "foreign" to others in their company, even when surrounded by people. Beginning just after Garrison's death, I remember sitting with detectives and attorneys and watching them attempt to be as professional as possible, while not letting themselves get too emotionally involved. I could have used a hug, and I felt very alone. When I walked down the street, people walking right past me, each of which have their own lives journey, with their own pain, their own fears, and their own struggles, and none of which give a crap about mine.

My walking through school and seeing many people that I know look directly into my eye, then turning away from me. Quite often they simply avoided me altogether. Their pain was too real, their fear of what I may say or do is too strong, or their insecurities are so monumental that they simply don't know what to do, or what to say.

My family and close friends needing to be there for me, to give me strength, and to listen to me, not knowing what to do. Their pain was real as well, and they needed for me to be there for them. I knew that they were hurting as well, and I didn't know if I had the strength to help them at all.

I remember one day, after a colleague saw me walking through campus, he deliberately turned around a corner, seemingly to avoid me. This was another example of how people around me were hurting. I went back to my office, and wrote an email to everyone in the District. I remember trying to say that I understand that everyone is experiencing pain, and that we don't know what to say or do. I suggested that if someone didn't know what to say, just come give me a hug. No words are necessary.

There for a short while, I got lots of hugs...

We are all scared, and we are all weak. We all look for strength in ourselves, and we look for strength in others. The strongest of us need someone stronger to give us strength. The weakest of us either look to others to bring out our inner strength, or we succumb to the realization that we either weak and/or choose not to be strong, or we are simply not strong enough. Some who appear weak are actually very strong, and discover that strength under the right circumstance. Some who are strong are actually very weak, and are just putting on a show to appear as if they are strong.

Some are truly strong...

Inner strength comes from a humble place. Inner strength comes from a confident place. Sometimes it's amazing what can "nudge" your inner strength into motion, and into action.

The loss of Garrison has humbled me in so many ways, and I could not imagine not having more empathy in others, as I do now.

There was an interesting nudge in the right direction for me...

The Woman in the Red Dress

One of the only instances where I was really upset with the Riverside County D.A.'s office came the week of the murder. I received a phone call asking me to bring Gregory in on Wednesday (two days after the murder) to speak with a child psychologist. I was told on the phone that I could be there with him during the interview, and they just wanted to see how he was doing. So I took Gregory, as I agreed. However, when I walked into the main entrance, I was informed that I couldn't be in the room with him. They just wanted to talk with him, alone.

Obviously, this makes sense, from their perspective. They wanted to talk to Gregory without me around, in the event that I was also a threat to Gregory's safety.

But...

I was furious, and I was very upset. I did not like being manipulated (from my perspective), and I did not like feeling as if Gregory was being taken away from me. I was leaving him with a complete stranger, and with someone with whom I had no sense of trust.

What would happen if they closed the doors, spoke with Gregory, then decided it was in his best interest not to see me again?

My helplessness and my frustration were indescribable. This was a very painful experience for me.

Once I was told what was going to happen, I instantly had to overcome my anger and resentment, I had to gather my strength, and I had to calmly walk Gregory into the examining room. I then fibbed to my son, telling him I had to go the restroom. I left him alone, with a stranger, and shutting that door on my way out was unbearable.

Walking away from him on that day was arguably one of the most difficult things I had ever done since finding my murdered son. I did not want to leave him with anyone, and I mean anyone, that I didn't know and trust implicitly. I was an emotional wreck, and I felt like a zombie. I slowly migrated outside of the D.A.'s office, where alongside of Main Street, there are multiple palm trees directly adjacent to the building. I walked right up to one palm tree, placed my right hand onto the tree, bowed my head, closed my eyes, and I cried. I couldn't stop. I just cried. It was probably more like sobbing, actually.

Then, from behind me, I heard a woman's voice. "Sir, are you ok?" I took a deep breath, attempted to wipe my face dry, and turned around to face her.

"I have had a tough week."

That is all I could muster as a response.

This woman, who in moments would become an angel to me, was standing there, in a red dress. I believe she worked inside the building, and was outside to have a cigarette. She looked me deep into the eyes, and asked bluntly "sir, did you lose a son?"

At that instant, I lost all emotional control. She gently approached me, put her arms around me, and gave me a huge hug. As I sobbed, she spoke to me. I can't recall specifically she said. However, this is a brief idea of what she said, and how she changed my life that day...

"Everyone you know, everyone who loves you, everyone who cares, will want to hug you. They will want to help you. They will want to love you. They will not know what to do. But please remember, they are suffering, they need you to be strong, and they need you to hug them, too."

Then she was gone.

I was struck by what she said. I don't even remember what she looks like. I just remember the red dress, her hug, and the powerful message of her words. She was gone, but she has no idea how much strength she gave me, by allowing me to be humble enough to know that *this isn't just about me.* This humble approach I adopted has impacted so many people, in so many ways, that I can't even imagine the ramifications.

Her words let me (to the dismay of many) ask "how are YOU doing?" Whenever I meet people, and they go through the "expected" mourning etiquette, and ask me their obligatory questions, they would always seem hesitant.

By my being able to be humble enough to ask "how are YOU doing?" allowed me to help others cope with *their* loss.

This may be hard to grasp, so please be patient. So many people, too numerous to count, have told me "I can't imagine what you are going through." That is undoubtedly true. However, the flip-side of that coin is also true. I have no idea what any one of my friends, any one of my colleagues, any one of my family or acquaintances has felt. I have NO idea what they have gone through, because of this tragedy.

"I have a hard time describing what I am going through. It is all so hard. How are you? Where were you, and what did you think when you first heard the news about Garrison?"

Whenever I asked this question, immediate reactions ranged from crying, to shaking, to complete stunned silence. People were dumbfounded when I asked them this question. They never expected my empathy for them, and never in a million years would they expect me to ask them to explain to me what they are feeling.

On many occasions, I don't think that many had the emotional strength to deal with their feelings – they were concerned with consoling me, with trying to be strong, and trying to help me feel better.

To anyone who never heard about Garrison's murder until this book, what did you think when you realized what this story was about? What did you think, as you started putting the pieces of this epic puzzle in place, and realized the severity of a mother murdering her infant child?

Perhaps this question hits everyone from the blind side.

That's ok.

They were right – no one knows precisely what I felt, or the range of emotions I experienced. Sometimes I feel I don't either. Conversely, I have no idea what anyone else experienced, as well.

To anyone who knew me when the murder happened, again think about what *you* experienced when *you* first heard of Garrison's murder. Your experience was just as real as mine, and your pain is no less intense or severe.

This beautiful person in the red dress helped me understand this. This woman in a red dress gave me so much strength. I would love to thank her, from the bottom of my heart. She gave me so much focus, and so much clarity. I needed that focus, and she shined a light onto my dark path.

She helped me be strong, so that I could heal through helping others in my life.

"Open House"

Inspired by the woman in the red dress, I decided to allow an "open house" for anyone who wished to come to begin healing. It was held the Saturday following Garrison's death.

This was a difficult decision in actuality. All I wanted to do was crawl into a hole, and hide from everyone and everything. But I do believe that, because of the strength I had gained from that woman in the red dress, that I now had the strength to help others who were hurting inside, and I desperately wanted to facilitate a feeling of community healing.

I told my family, close friends and colleagues that I would welcome anyone who wished to come by my house and that my door would "be open" anytime that day. Anyone was welcome. It was a time for all of us to digest what had happened. I asked a few people for help, and they took care of all preparations.

Little did I know the numbers of people who would show up on that special day.

My colleagues in my department brought more food than would be needed to feed a small army. The nursing department came en-mass with all of the love you could imagine. My family, my friends, my colleagues, many of my students, people whom I had barely known, and people whom I had never met – all converged on that house, on that beautiful day.

The day was a blur emotionally, and in my memory, and I can still only vaguely remember who was there. I remember certain faces, certain moments, and I remember certain conversations. I remember everyone from my department coming, and the arm loads of food. I remember Scott's huge basket of gifts, and I think of it every time I look at the basket, which is used every day. I remember so much, and I am thankful for so much. There is so much I have a hard time remembering as well.

On that emotional day, the one thing that I tried very hard to do (and it was extremely difficult for me) was to spend *quality time in conversation* with anyone who wanted to talk. I remember the first person I spoke with, the young daughter of one of my colleagues at RCC. When her family walked into the room, and I saw the look on her face when she looked up to me, I picked her up, and gave her a huge hug. We both started crying. I then sat on the floor of the living room, and gave her everything I had. I asked her about what she is thinking, I asked her how she first heard what happened, I asked her if she was mad, I asked her if she could sleep. I hit her with every question that I was in fact asking myself. I remember being so focused on our conversation that I realized I was ignoring everyone else, but to be honest, I didn't care, because it just didn't matter. My focus was on that moment, my focus was on her feelings, and this focus seemed to me at that moment to be the most important thing in my life.

I started moving around, talking with many people. Pulling them aside, generally on the back porch, sitting, listening, crying, and trying to share whatever strength I could muster.

When I decided to open up my house, I didn't know what to expect. What I realized is that I actually opened up my heart. I gave everyone a chance to open their hearts, share their pain, and focus on what the future may hold.

I was told later by family members that I had seemed to be ignoring people. I sincerely hope that this wasn't the case. It took all of my strength, and all of my will, to make sure that anyone who wanted to share quality time with me could. It wasn't easy at all…

Missing The Links

I am so glad that we all got together that day.

People often find it hard to cordially receive honest gifts of others, and on that day I found it hard to cordially receive honest gifts from others. People bearing gifts during times of grief, is a far different experience than on other occasions, like birthdays or holidays such as Christmas. I felt obligated to return the favor, but knew that wasn't acceptable. Part of my grief recovery was in allowing others to give from their hearts and my open acceptance of these gifts.

Sometimes baking a cake is the best thing a person can do. Sometimes this is the best way that someone can express their pain. Sometimes life is as simple as a good piece of pie.

There were so many examples of friends and colleagues offering help. So many invitations for me and Gregory to come to their homes for quiet dinners. Friends asking us to join them on small trips – Joshua Tree, Palm Springs aerial tramway, riding horses. There were so many people coming over to my house for visits, bringing wonderful food, drinking lots of wine, and allowing ourselves to cry and to laugh.

Just one example – the nursing department at RCC is filled with many good-hearted people. They took the initiative of organizing dinners for me and Gregory. For many weeks after Garrison died, there was a constant stream of people coming in and out of my house, bringing gifts of food from their heart.

I blame them for my gaining weight during this time!

I think what I found difficult is not succumbing to my natural instinct, which was to lock my door. I had to swallow my pride, to a certain extent. I had to let all of these good-hearted people share their pain with me.

I also learned that sometimes life can be as simple as a good friend not accepting "no" for an answer.

The day after Garrison died, Steve Jordahl and I were at my home, when all of a sudden there was a knock at the front door. It was Sylvia Thomas, a senior administrator at my college. There she was, with tremendous emotional pain on her face. She came into my home, and gave me a hug – a very long hug. She asked what she could do. I gave her some blabbering answer of how there was little she could do, but she wouldn't accept it.

She marched right past me, and began straightening up the kitchen. She washed dishes, she cleaned counters – she just took over. She did this over my objections, and she did this with tremendous love and compassion in her heart.

By the time she was done, this house was presentable for what would be a very hectic week.

I will be forever grateful to Sylvia for that gesture. For the next year, we would talk religiously, and continuously. She was a shoulder for me, and I am forever grateful for her.

Sylvia is just one example, of countless friends and colleagues who stepped through that door in the next weeks. She is just one example of someone for whom I am forever grateful, and I tear up thinking about how hard this must have been for everyone, and how thankful I truly am.

Garrison's Memorial

I hate funerals. I always have. I can't think of anyone who would ever say that they "love" funerals, but most people can deal with them in their own way, and usually find the strength to attend.

Since Garrison passed, I have not found the strength to attend funerals at all.

I remember as a child, a family friend had passed away. I remember looking around at everyone's faces, and seeing their pain. I also remember someone, I don't remember who, making a comment regarding the widow. The widow wasn't crying, and the comments I overheard were quite harsh and judgmental, implying that the widow obviously didn't care about her husband.

Expectations...

How you should grieve, how you should react, how you should feel. Expectations are tough to handle, and tough to swallow.

You may find people often overtly judging you, based on *their* expectations of how *you* should act, and how *you* should feel.

It was expected for us to have a funeral for Garrison. I had so many people asking about it.

I wanted nothing to do with it. What I wanted was to be inclusive to people, to be inclusive to their pain and suffering, and to be inclusive to the collective sense of loss. I felt I had already done that at our "open house" the weekend after Garrison had died. I have always felt, and I still do, that close interpersonal communications and conversations are the best way to help the grieving process. Having and organized gathering, on some levels, is counter-productive.

However, there is something to be said about a collective gathering, in order to share with many people your sadness over loss.

I feared that Garrison's funeral may turn into a "show" or fiasco publicly. I wasn't interested in drawing attention to myself. I just wanted the people who felt the sadness and loss personally to come, hug each other, laugh, smile, cry, eat, drink, relax – and breathe.

I now get sickened when I see people, parading themselves in front of a camera, for their five minutes of fame, when they have tragically lost a loved one. I am absolutely sickened by this, on so many levels.

It is only about them, and the cameras pointed towards their hunger for attention.

My heart is saddened when I see people pleading for the return of a loved one, or for information leading towards the capture or arrest for a violent crime. This must be done. Parasitic "attention getters" grotesque me more now than they ever did. How pathetic they are.

So what should I do? How can I publicly pay respect to Garrison, appease the need for others to grieve, so that they can get on with their lives?

Someone suggested "how about a celebration of life?"

I hate titles like "celebration of life" even if it is the best description possible. It was hard for me – Garrison' was only 17 months old, and had yet to truly begin his life. It is hard to celebrate this fact.

Nothing we came up with fit what I was feeling. Nothing we came up with described what I wanted, or how I felt. We decided on a "memorial" for Garrison, but even that title didn't satisfy me. It still doesn't.

I knew that I needed help in order to pull this off, and I asked my sister Timeree to handle the details and arrangements for me, but I wanted to make the major decisions including what the themes would be.

First and foremost – where could I gather the people that would be the most impacted by Garrison's loss, in a place that was convenient, private, and most comfortable for the majority of people in attendance? I decided to geographically place the memorial halfway between where I lived (which would accommodate most of my colleagues) and where I grew up (which would accommodate close friends and family).

My Uncle Gene suggested that I speak to Mike and Hennie Monteleone, lifelong friends and colleagues of our family. They had built a beautiful home on beautifully landscaped acreage where they host weddings and celebrations, called Monteleone Meadows in Temecula (subliminal plug intended). I gathered the courage to ask them if we could meet, and when I met with them, they met me with open arms. I cannot express my gratitude enough. Mike and Hennie accommodated a convenient date (Saturday, March 14), on very short notice. Their property was absolutely beautiful, spacious, and comfortable. There was plenty of *space* for people to sit, either in groups, or in isolation.

I was concerned with giving everyone the most relaxing environment possible, and I knew there would be many children there, so I arranged for lots of entertainment for the children. I asked the ECS program at RCC if I could hire some of their staff and interns, to keep children occupied and entertained. We set aside a large fenced off area for children to play – we brought in inflatable jumpers, had face-painters, jugglers, and many other activities to keep children entertained.

I felt this was important, because I wanted parents to be able to let their children play, be supervised and safe, so that they be able to take their minds of them, in order to relax. This was one of my best ideas, and it was quite successful. I feel that this was one of the best things I did through all of this.

I asked Terry Shaw, a colleague and friend of mine from RCC, to speak to the audience for me. This was an easy choice. I wanted someone who wasn't a family member. I wanted someone who was articulate with his words, and I wanted someone who would offer a calming message. I also wanted someone that I hadn't burdened so much by me with Garrison's passing. There were many people that would have been splendid, had I asked them for their help.

I was honored that Terry accepted my invitation.

I did muster the strength to say a few words, which was not my intent, but a few people suggested that I do so. I tried to keep it simple, and convey my thankfulness to everyone who "came together" in this time of tragedy, and how we gave each other strength. I don't remember exactly what I said.

It ended up being a beautiful day, and I am so thankful that I was able to allow my sister Timeree to make it something that I won't forget. It was a good day for healing, for me, and for everyone. It was a good day for remembrance. And it was a good day for strength.

Many people told me it was the most beautiful "funeral" they had ever been to…

I guess I will take this as a compliment.

A Second Tragedy

It is often said, that in life, bad news comes in "threes." Garrison's murder was a major trauma, suffered by so many people. In particular, the staff at RCC's ECS was emotionally shaken, and exhausted. The other parents and families whose children attended were emotionally shaken. It was a tragedy in this small community, and this community was in pain, and the wound was still very much open.

But another tragedy befell our ECS community, almost exactly one month after Garrison's death. Out of respect for the family that was involved, I will keep some specific details private.

A classmate of Gregory's had an older sister who was killed in a violent car crash. She was riding in a car with some friends, and had stopped at a four-way intersection, each with a stop sign. They proceeded to drive through, and drunk driver hit their car from the side at full speed.

She was a beautiful teenager, having her entire life in front of her. Good in school, never getting into serious trouble, a good big sister, a loving daughter – all of the things anyone could ever want in a teenage daughter. She had a bright future, and her loss was (and is) tragic for the family.

This second tragedy had two affects. Firstly, and most obvious, was the impact on the family. As with Garrison's loss, the second impact was on our ECS community, of which I am including Gregory and me.

When their daughter died, I didn't know what to do. It was only a month or so since Garrison's passing. I was still very much in shock, and in a persistent state of numbness. Going to and from the ECS, dropping Gregory off or picking him up, was one of the daily routines I had to work through, and make myself get this done. I was barely able to do this, and it took a tremendous amount of strength on my part. When this young girl died, obviously, I would see the family and Gregory's friend on a regular basis. Just like most people, and especially with what had recently happened to me, I didn't know what to say, or what to do.

How ironic – I was now placed in the same position, at the same time, as everyone "hovering" over and around me. I tried hard not to "hover" with this family, but let them know I was there for them, if they would like.

The news hit the ECS community very hard, having two tragedies within a month. The mood of the community was solemn, at best. I remember one occasion of seeing Lynne Vazquez, and she was having a very hard time keeping herself together emotionally. She told me that she couldn't take it anymore, and that she didn't know if she could continue.

I remember sitting with her, and becoming very stern. I told her how important she was, and how important what she did was. I tried to emphasize her impact on Gregory, on his life, and on mine. I reminded her of all of the work that she had done, bringing in professional help, coordinating so many aspects of Gregory's care, and continuing to provide a safe, nurturing and caring environment for not only Gregory, but everyone else there.

I told Lynne that she needed to stay strong. She needed to continue doing what was so important, even more than she might realize. I was very serious during this discussion, but she needed to know her impact on my life, and that she was also needed by the other families especially after this second tragedy. It was her eyes, watching over Gregory daily, surrounding him with people who had nothing but his best interests at heart, which was I needed most desperately.

The mother of the accident victim and I didn't talk for quite a while. Sometimes we just wouldn't see one another. Other times, when I saw her, we avoided one another. It was gut-wrenching for me to see her or her family. I can easily imagine it being the same for her.

However, one day when I was coming out of the offices, she was about a hundred feet away walking towards me. Our eyes met, and instantly I knew that we both were ready to connect with one another. We shared a very long quiet hug, with lots of tears. I remember telling her how very sorry I was for her loss. I remember her telling me about her daughter's loss, her losing her best friend, and how her entire purpose in life was lost in an instant.

As I sit here writing this I realized that I never had that same feeling. I never questioned whether my life now had purpose, since Garrison died.

Other things were discussed, much of which I can't remember. But one aspect of this conversation I will remember for the rest of my life.

She told me how much she respected me. I was stunned. Me, of all people, she admired? She told me that she and her family had watched me from a distance since Garrison died. She saw how I handled the media, she saw how I got help for my family, and she saw how I moved forward every day, no matter how badly I was hurting.

She told me that watching me from afar helped her to deal with her loss.

What a compliment. I was absolutely blown away.

Since that day, I have reached out to her multiple times. I offered to let our kids spend time together. I offered to sit with her and talk, and to help in any way I could. We did speak a couple of times on the phone. I sincerely wanted to reach out, but I think it was too much of an uncomfortable situation for her, and her family. I have even seen her at public functions, and we give each other respectful space.

The last time I saw her was at a candlelight memorial for victims of crime here in Riverside County. I wanted to walk up and say hi. I didn't. I gave her the space that rightly she deserves.

She didn't know I was there...

I am so sorry for her loss, and her pain. I wish she would have allowed me to help a little bit more. I like to think I could have helped, at least a little bit. Perhaps I could have helped pull some of that unbearable weight off of her shoulders, to give her some strength to help her rebuild her life.

My Focus: Dealing with Lori's family and friends.

I have often felt like I am in a bad position. How do I share my pain, and my bewilderment, with those who are in Lori's life? When Garrison was murdered, I reached out to Lori's family and friends. I didn't blame them, and I honestly felt their pain. Obviously, Steve and his family were instrumental in helping me. Their importance in my life is unquestioned. I also opened my door to Lori's aunts and uncles, mother, and brother. This was in addition to Lori's multiple friends, and various colleagues at her school.

Missing The Links

"Opening my door" is not an exaggeration. I gave sets of keys to my door, so that they could come and go, when convenient. I tried to make them very comfortable, and included them in our pain and misery.

However, and sadly, it is the bad aspects of this openness that my memory is focused. I was extremely angry, and continue to be so today.

Lori has an Aunt and Uncle, and I remember that Lori often gave me advice, based on her own experience, for me never to trust them. She was quite blunt, as a matter of fact. In her opinion, they had lied, manipulated, cheated and stole their way throughout their lives. I personally know of examples since I met Lori where this had happened. They were among the first to show up at my door, within a day of Garrison's death. My biggest mistake was to be so friendly and open with them.

I find it funny how I didn't heed Lori's advice, and how it bit me in the ass.

How interesting it is when families quickly go after one another, when someone with wealth or possession dies. How quickly do family members converge on a house, and then all of a sudden, artifacts are "missing."

Lori's Aunt and Uncle stole from me, in more ways than one. They ransacked my house when I wasn't there. They went through everything, either with intent to steal, or to satisfy some sick morbid curiosity to intrude on intimate aspects of my life. They searched through Lori's computer files. They told the Public Defender's Office that I was going to be a "hostile witness." They spoke with the media about topics which they were in fact, ignorant. Evidently they were speaking with publishers on how to sell Lori's story. I distinctly remember one evening when Lori's Uncle had obviously consumed a large quantity of cocaine, yelling and screaming at me about not spending everything I had in order to defend Lori. He swore he would do whatever it took to get her out of jail. He was very belligerent, accosting, and rude.

I shut him down that night, and I cringe with anger at my stupidity, in even allowing them to enter my house the way I did. My last memory of their "visit" was their leaving my house, with a car load of my belongings, which I didn't realize until *after* they had left.

Although I am so proud of how I conducted myself after Garrison's murder, in so many aspects of my life, that I brought in people I trusted, and I tried to think rationally. However, this is one example of how my "heart" opened up to someone that I shouldn't have. I was somewhat weak, and this should be a good lesson for any reader.

There are other examples. Good friends of Lori who had borrowed money when they were desperate, and to whom I no longer exist. They stole from me, as well. Good colleagues and friends of Lori from her work, who I sincerely thought were friends of mine and Gregory's, who stopped returning my phone calls.

So many doors were shut from this part of my life's journey.

Fortunately, others were opened as well.

My Focus: The Trial and the Public Arena.

Big Government. You often hear complaints about our government, and that it is too large and unmanageable. In many cases, these complaints are completely justified.

In my personal case, there is one aspect to this "bloated" bureaucracy that immediately stepped in, and helped me tremendously. I do not know what I would have done without these dedicated professionals.

The Riverside County's District Attorney's Office has a division dedicated to victims of crime called the Division of Victim's Services. Its mission statement expresses that it "empowers victims and witnesses of crime through advocacy and support services while promoting successful prosecution."

Victim Services instantly came to me, and explained how they could help. I remember how they arranged for psychological help for me and Gregory, and attempted to do the same for Nick. They also guided me through the legal process. They shielded me from the media, and provided protective mechanisms in multiple ways. They (unwittingly) gave me a formal education on the legal system, patiently answering my many questions. They also especially helped with regard to the courtroom. I could be escorted into and out of the courtroom, could be escorted to press conferences, etc. They coordinated with *The Unforgettables Foundation*, a charitable organization which graciously paid for Garrison's cremation.

Kym Conover. I cannot express my gratitude to her and her staff. Their professionalism, their expertise, and the personal nature that they conducted themselves cannot be over-emphasized.

Big government. This is an example of how taxes are collected, and how monies are spent, in ways that most of "us" are completely unaware.

Some will still argue, however, that it shouldn't be spent at all. I humbly disagree.

How would I ever know, beforehand, how desperately I would need these services?

The greatest gift that Kym's office brought to my life was stability, and someone I that I knew I could count on. They shielded my family to a large extent, especially in the public arena. Try to imagine having six news vans sitting outside your door. Imagine every move you make being filmed. Imagine having everyone close all windows and window shades, so that cameras can't follow your every move inside of your house.

The D.A.'s office told me that I was free to speak with the media. They would not tell me who I could speak with, or what I could say. They did have some advice, however. They asked me to be very careful on what precisely I would say. They made sure that I realized that everything that I said could have repercussions on the entire legal process, or on how the potential jury may view the case.

Every word I would say would be filmed or published, frozen in time, perhaps misquoted or more importantly misconstrued, and would be taken very seriously by everyone who "listened" to this misinformation.

This reality struck me. I remember in the days immediately following Garrison's death, one of the first things that Steve really helped me with was with the media. When they would come to the door, he would answer the door and kindly tell them that I had no comment.

We were contacted by three nationally broadcast shows. I was offered payment and trips to the beautiful cities around the nation that hosted the shows. My story indeed garnered national attention and interest, and the public wanted to hear more about this tragedy.

However, I respectfully declined each offer, simply saying that I wasn't ready emotionally to speak about the case yet.

Meanwhile, there were two things that had been evolving that troubled me greatly at the time. The first was photographs of Garrison suddenly appearing in the media. I hadn't realized at the time that one of the extended family members had (unknowingly to me) made a shrine using many personal artifacts and photographs of Garrison that they had removed (again unknowingly to me) from my house. Once the shrine was placed outside, obviously the media recorded its images. I know that this was done from a good place, but I was very upset, and I felt extremely violated.

Secondly, the reports in the media morphed from what was known as fact at the time, to speculation of what had happened. There was one report, which became widely disseminated, regarding Nick's possible participation in the murder. There were other reports questioning why he didn't stop his mother.

I couldn't take it anymore. It really bothers me when intelligent people (including myself) make "decisions," or base their opinions, on factually incorrect information.

I told Steve that I had to talk with the media. We slowly walked outside of the house. I didn't say a word to anyone. I simply looked up towards the news vans, and the crews of people that surrounded them. That was all that they needed. Upon making eye contact with them, they immediately converged on me, meeting me on the street.

I spoke about the pain my family was experiencing. I spoke about the request to respect our privacy throughout this process. I spoke about how I had always supported my wife, and how I didn't understand why this happened. I spoke about the need to let the legal process finish, and to look at all of the facts in their entirety, before we make our final judgments.

I attempted to shift the focus the main attention of the media away from Nick, and in my opinion, it worked to a great degree.

The entire time, Steve stood next to me. On several occasions, I was having difficulty keeping my composure. My knees got weak, and I felt dizzy. I felt Steve's hand on my back – giving me support. That is something that I will forever be grateful – the strength he continued to give me.

That was it. That turned out to be the only time I ever spoke to the media during that time, with the exception of one newspaper reporter for the Press Enterprise, the local newspaper here in Riverside. Not even on the day of Lori's sentencing – when I walked immediately past the television reporters reporting live on the sentencing for her conviction of first-degree murder of our son, Garrison.

I thought it was strange. I would have expected at least one question of how I felt about the conviction or sentencing. I am not sure how I would have reacted, or what answers I would have provided. But to walk by these television reporters, escorted by Kym Conover, look them directly in the eye, and not have a glimmer of recognition to me evidence that what I had wanted all along had indeed worked.

This came as a surprise to Kym as well.

I guess my not grabbing my "five minutes" of attention had an impact on whether I was recognized or not.

I would like to make mention on the professionalism of the media, in my case. During the weeks following the murder, the media was extremely respectful. They did their job, and were persistent trying to get any information that they could, but I never felt as if they were overly aggressive, nor did I feel that they "invaded my space" as I would have expected them to do. It was probably a combination of the personnel that were assigned to my case, and how my family and I handled the media. No matter what the situation was, I am appreciative of how the media handled itself in the days following the murder.

Investigations

Contradictions. I found that I was placed into many different positions, emotionally, when it came to the pre-trial investigations. The detectives and the District Attorney look for any information leading to the conviction of Lori. The Public Defender's Office looks for any information leading to Lori being found not guilty, or criminally not responsible for Garrison's death. Most people realize this contrast. I find it interesting that any information the prosecution discovers *must* be given to defense counsel, even it if isn't going to be used at trial. If investigators for the prosecution discover evidence that may call into question Lori's guilt, and possibly exonerate her, they are required to give this to the defense. However, the same is not true for defense counsel. If the defense counsel investigators discover any new evidence which would lead towards Lori's conviction, they are under no obligation to provide this evidence to the prosecution. They are under no obligation to help the prosecution. This is how, in practice, the total burden of proof lies with the prosecution.

I was interviewed by both prosecution and defense counsel investigators. I was asked multiple questions, from multiple perspectives, on multiple occasions.

I didn't want to help the defense. To some extent, this is hard to admit, especially to myself. Being as angry with Lori as I was, I found that I when I spoke with the defense investigators I was, naturally, very guarded and careful in how I spoke.

I was not, however, a "hostile" witness, as was implied by Lori's Uncle and Aunt. I was truthful and honest with defense counsel. I didn't hide anything from them, and I did my best to be of assistance.

I just didn't feel enthusiastic about helping them do their jobs.

The Trial

Waiting. Being patient. Letting the "system" take its course.

This was extremely difficult. However, with all things in consideration (and in hindsight), my experience was quite typical.

It was just over two years after Garrison's murder when the trial officially began. I was told that it would take a while, but this seemed to me like a very long time. However, as I listened to other families who had somewhat similar circumstances, I learned that many trials took upwards of five years to begin. So I guess that two years wasn't that long.

Missing The Links

Most things in life are simply about perspective.

Many court days. Many hearings and meetings. Delay, upon delay.

It is easy to see how people get so upset at the process. It is easy to see the frustration, the anguish, and the need for closure. Most of this, however, is due to *our* expectations, as victims, most of which are unreasonable. I found it most helpful to keep it in perspective, and this helped me to deal with the delays.

As I have mentioned, I sat back and watched three different prosecuting Assistant D.A.'s assigned to Lori's case. I hated not having "consistency" in the prosecution, and in having a feeling like Lori's case was being passed from person to person. Will Robinson was eventually assigned Lori's case as prosecuting attorney, and I am fortunate that he ended up with her case.

There were many aspects of the trial that both intrigued me, and made me quite frustrated.

I was banned from all court proceedings, except when I had to testify. I understand the basic rationale for this – I was a prime witness, and I could not be allowed to have any aspect of my testimony swayed by any other testimony. It was extremely difficult for me. There were some details I would have not wanted to know about, especially those dealing with the forensic aspects of Garrison's death. I don't know if I could have observed that testimony. But I would have greatly appreciated the chance to observe the testimony detailing Lori's psychological state, the details of how her life took a downward spiral (from the legal perspective), the arguments for and against her medical versus criminal insanity, the testimony by the expert witnesses, and the testimony of other friends or family.

There are many aspects of this case that I was very much interested in learning more about.

I felt so ignorant during the trial, and I felt so helpless.

Lori had made the interesting decision to not be present for any court proceedings, which was her legal right. There are good and bad aspects of this. Had she been in the courtroom during the testimony, she could have seen first-hand the devastation she caused (this is probably why she didn't want to be there). She also could have helped in her defense, especially for aspects of testimony that she wouldn't agree with.

One good thing about her not being there was that people were not forced to visually confront her, especially her son Nick. I am thankful for that, for Nick's sake.

In my experience, being under intense scrutiny during my testimony was difficult. Try to imagine yourself sitting on a witness stand, testifying against a loved one. Imagine being interrogated from differing angles, and not being allowed to answer fully. I was admonished multiple times by the presiding judge for how I was answering questions.

What an interesting mix of emotions, intellect, exhaustion and stress. The trial was all of this, and so much more.

For me the trial had many aspects that I found quite intriguing. Intellectually speaking, I had to first get a grasp on the legal process, and then I had to deal with being kept "out of the loop" most often. Trying to comprehend how an insanity defense works, what is "insane" from a criminal perspective, what testimony would be used, what would be excluded, what was being said (and by whom), and how the jury was reacting to the testimony. These were all difficult questions and concerns that I had.

From an emotional standpoint, just not knowing was extremely difficult, and not being able to be a part of what was happening was even worse. Sitting in the waiting room immediately adjacent to the courtroom, day after day, was excruciating. Not being at the courthouse, day after day, was torture.

Waiting for phone calls, even for just a brief update, was excruciating. These days were amongst the worst.

I was juggling the trial, dealing with family and friends, coordinating information with people across the country, and I was trying to work as well.

We live in interesting times...

Attending Testimony

I wasn't allowed to attend any testimony during the trial. However, the trial was open to the public. There were two people who were in attendance at almost every court session, and in retrospect this was extremely important to me. One was a colleague and friend of mine from school, and the other was a life-long friend and mentor of Lori's.

Judy Haugh is a wonderful friend of mine, whom I met at RCC. She has also become an "aunt" to Gregory, and is very special in his life as well. We had grown close as friends when both her father and mine passed away around the same time. We knew each other by serving on committees together, and she had recently retired from the school district. During the trial, she had the chance to be at all hearings and testimony.

Marj Rust, in my mind, was Lori's mother/grandmother. They had known each other for a very long time, and Marj was a consistent source of advice and support in Lori's life. Lori didn't have that from anyone else. When Lori murdered Garrison, Marj was just as devastated as anyone by what Lori did. Marj was wonderful, and I am very thankful for her perspective. Lori trusted her enough to give her authority over her financial and legal matters, of which she has never acted in any way, other than in Lori's best interest. Marj's experiences through this ordeal would be worthy of her writing a book as well.

Marj lived in Colorado, and couldn't afford to fly down and stay for the entire trial. There were times when the Defense counsel or the D.A.'s office would assist her with some expenses, but this help didn't cover all of her expenses. When the main part of the trial began, I arranged to have a fifth-wheel recreational vehicle travel trailer available to her, so that she wouldn't have to worry about accommodations. I wanted to help as much as I could.

I valued Marj's perspective. She acted in Lori's behalf, but also helped Gregory and me immensely. She was a "conduit" between Lori's interests and mine. She is Lori's best advocate. I trusted that when she shared something with me, it was truthful. I never felt that she took advantage of anything, from my perspective.

When it came to my family, I wanted to be as inclusive as possible, but I also felt strongly that there were some aspects of the trial that I didn't want them to witness firsthand. When I knew that specific details of Garrison's murder would be presented, I expressed to my family that it was my opinion that they shouldn't be there. I really didn't want them to see the photos, and hear the medical and scientific evidence. But, I also made sure that they knew that it was their decision.

There was one aspect of the case that I felt very strongly that they shouldn't be present and that was during specific parts of my testimony. I knew that my testimony would deal greatly with the relationship that Lori and I had. There would be specific of her relationship with my family, her anger issues, and my "failures" as her husband. I just didn't feel comfortable having my mother and sisters present for that part of the testimony. I felt that there would be things said that they frankly shouldn't hear. I didn't want them to be present while I was forced to "air my dirty laundry" on the witness stand. I put my foot down for this, and I am very glad that I did. However, my family was quite upset with me. I hope they realize that I did it for their benefit as well. It's not that I was embarrassed by what was said – I knew it was part of the public record, and I also knew that anyone else could be there. Marj and Judy would be present. But my relationship with some of my family had been strained anyway, and I didn't want to add to this. This was a desperate time for healing, not for opening up old wounds.

Thankfully, my family respected my wishes.

My Focus: Confronting Garrison's Murderer

After Lori was convicted, and during the sanity phase of the trial, I forced myself to have many "casual" conversations with Gregory on whether he would like to see his mother. Sometimes he would simply say no. Sometimes he would say that he would like to see her. On those rare occasions he said he would like to visit her, I would ask him what he would say. His responses ranged from anger and pain, to how much he missed her.

Each time we talked about what he wanted to say, Gregory cried.

I made a decision, based on advice from Gregory's therapist (and a few others whom I trusted very much), that Gregory should see his mother. I knew in my heart this was the right thing to do. This was strictly in Gregory's best interest, but it went against my core. It went against every paternal protective mechanism that I had.

I did not want to do this, but it wasn't about me now, was it?

I wonder if most people, in my position, could think this way...

The basic rationale was this – Gregory had not seen his mother in two years. He was angry over what his mother had done. He missed his mother. He missed his brother. He had so much pain, so much anger, and so much frustration.

This little man had to tell his mother what he felt – good or bad.

Believe me, this took tremendous focus, on my part.

Since the trial had started, based on this advice, I had been pondering whether to take Gregory to see his mother or not. It had been weighing terribly on my mind. However, with the trial's end, and with Lori's conviction, there was a deadline to the legal process looming. If I had waited any longer, I would have had to take Gregory to see her in prison. At least at that time, she was still in Riverside.

In addition, I had procrastinated far too long. Gregory was growing, he was changing, and he needed to do this. Time may heal all wounds, but time also distorts the memory of what actually happened, distorts feelings about what happened, and distorts reactions.

Prior to taking Gregory to see Lori, there were only a couple of people who knew about my contemplating this. In each case, the initial reaction was of shock, as it should have been. But after thoughtful conversation, the realization that it was the right thing to do would set in. I didn't have the strength to continue defending my decision with everyone, so I kept it from most everyone.

I needed to be strong. I needed to make sure that this visit was only for Gregory's best interest. I felt strongly that taking Gregory to visit Lori, unannounced, wasn't the right thing to do. I would have to visit her first. I needed to set the stage for Gregory's visit, and I needed to set the ground rules.

So there I found myself signing in to visit Lori in the holding facility in downtown Riverside. This was the first time I had been inside of this building.

Since the day of Garrison's murder, on two prior occasions I had felt weak, and had the sudden overpowering urge to visit Lori. This feeling of helplessness, anger and despair seemed overpowering. On the first occasion, I wanted to drive to see her, but I didn't. The second occasion was when I came out of the victim services unit at the District Attorney's offices, which are immediately adjacent to the holding facility where Lori was. As I walked out towards the street, I saw this building and I had seen dozens of times, knowing that Lori was there. When I saw that building on that day, I felt the sudden urge to see her. On this day I was angry, and I felt I needed to see her. Instead of walking towards my parked truck, I walked towards the building entrance. I suddenly stopped, and I didn't go inside. I don't know if it was my strength, my weakness, my being scared, or my being so damned angry, but something kept me from going inside. I am glad that I didn't that day. I don't think that a visit that day would have gone well for me. I wouldn't have been in control.

This time was different, however. This was about Gregory. I had to be very strong, and I had to maintain my focus, in his best interest. This helped me tremendously...

So there I sat, in the waiting area, watching and listening to many people who were trying to see their loved ones in jail. What an odd feeling. It seemed like an eternity sitting there, sitting there all alone except with my own thoughts.

I don't know for a fact that this is the case, but when I was signing in, it seemed that the Sheriff who signed me in was startled by my stating who I was, and who I was there to see. It is reasonable to expect a small community of people in those facilities, where most inmates are known by most of the staff that actually take care of them. Lori's case was quite unique, and I am quite sure most inside that facility were familiar with the case, or knew her personally. She had been in this holding facility almost two years, and that is a long time.

My name was called. I was checked for weapons, and was allowed proceed to the elevator. I was carefully directed as to what to do, and then I was alone again, in an elevator, going up to the fifth floor. The elevator doors opened, and there was a small room with perhaps six small round chairs, each attached to the floor, looking at plate glass partitions, where the inmate would be led in. A very sterile environment. There were small black phone receivers to speak through the glass. I have seen this scene many times in movies and on television, but the sterile reality, including all of the sounds and smells of that moment, were very stark and startling to me.

I was still so alone. The room was completely empty. There were no other visitors in that room. There were no other inmates. There were no Sheriff Deputies in the room. I was alone, and it seemed like a very long time that I was there alone.

Alone except for the cameras which followed my every move. I remember being very much aware that everything that I said, everything that I did, and everything that happened would be witnessed by many people. That actually helped me to be strong during this visit.

Then I heard doors slamming. I heard voices. And there she was, being lead into the visiting room. This woman I both love and hate. This woman who was such a brutal killer, a psychopathic and delusional killer, and yet a person whom I pity very much.

She sat down, and picked up the receiver. I picked up mine. She bluntly asked how I was doing.

I don't remember my answer. I do recall staring at this woman, whom I had married, feeling both rage and sadness, simultaneously. I was so damned angry, but I also knew that I had to keep it cool.

This was all about Gregory.

It was all about Gregory. I remember discovering at the trial that she had assumed Gregory was to be home on that fateful day, and that she was surprised to discover that I had taken him to school.

Had he been home…

Had I lost him too…

She talked at length about how sorry she was. She repeated how much of a sense of loss she felt, and how she threw her life away. She tried to reassure me that she was the "normal" Lori that I had known, and that she was *much better now*.

I remember her expressing optimism in having her conviction overturned on appeal. She was convinced that the Judge made terrible mistakes in the trial, and that the jury hadn't come to the right conclusion. She also expressed her will to come home, once her conviction was overturned. She wanted her family back. She said that she wouldn't blame me for saying "no," but that she hoped I would allow her to come home and help rebuild our family.

I sat there in stunned silence as she said these words.

I remember thinking so many conflicting thoughts, sitting there shaking inside, biting my lip to keep from speaking what was truly on my mind.

I was never conflicted on whether she could come "home." That has never, ever, entered my mind. As I have mentioned previously, I was completely in fear of her getting out, and somehow getting access to Gregory. I knew I could *never* trust her again, under *any* circumstance.

But I kept my thoughts quiet.

One of the things that I do recall her repeating is something along the lines of…

"You know I am a good mother. No mother in her right mind would do such a thing."

Good point…

My thought process was something like "you are absolutely right. No one in their right mind would do such a thing. Yet you pleaded criminal insanity as a defense, and you think that you are perfectly fine right now. No need for additional treatment. No need for therapy. You think everything is back to normal. You feel that you are getting out of jail soon, and that you are coming home."

She is ok now. There is nothing wrong with her, and she is back to being her old self. She was crazy then, but she is ok now.

Yet she had consistently refused any medical treatment, or sought any psychological treatment for her "previous" mental condition.

She kept trying to convince me that she was a good mother, and that she wanted to come home.

This is how I segued into telling her that I wanted to bring Gregory. When I told her that I wanted her to see Gregory, she instantly pulled physically back (away from the glass), and said that she couldn't see him – she wouldn't see him.

I pulled out the *"good mother card."*

"If you think you are such a good mother, then you need to see him. He needs to see you, and tell you what he is thinking. This is important, and it is about Gregory, not you or me."

This is one of the few times in our lives that I believe she actually took my opinion seriously. After a few minutes of consideration, she agreed to see Gregory.

Remember that she could have, at any time, refused to see someone, including during the check-in process. I had to make sure that she would agree to see Gregory.

During this conversation, I felt that she attempted to manipulate me. I felt as if she were trying to sway my thoughts, even from behind her shield of glass. She kept trying to sway the conversation to topics she wanted to discuss, for example our relationship. She mentioned that she wished that I was a stronger man. She told me that I could see this coming, and that I didn't reach out to help her.

In my opinion, she was implying that if I were a stronger man, we wouldn't have gone through all of this.

I bit my lip.

Focus. This was about Gregory, and not about us.

I kept re-focusing our conversation.

I had to maintain my focus...

Gregory's Visit

Lori was scheduled to be sentenced on a Friday (her birthday – how ironic), and I decided to take Gregory that week. I made up a story to get Gregory out of the house, telling him that we were going to get a cheeseburger, and that we could go for a drive. As we were driving away from the house, my heart was racing. I will never forget this drive.

I hadn't just introduced this young man to the idea of seeing his mother that evening. I had been asking him questions, bringing up his mother, and asking him about his feelings for well over a month.

On this particular evening, the conversation went something like...

"Would you like to see your mother someday?"

"Yes," he said.

"What would you say to her?" I asked.

"I would tell her how mad I am at her. I would tell her I miss my baby Garrison."

A few moments of silence…

"Would you like to see her tonight?"

As I looked into the mirror, a shocked and stunned look on his face.

I will never forget it. This little five-year old boy, looking directly at me in my rear-view mirror, in shock, with the reality that he could indeed see her.

"No, I don't want to see her."

This was the first time he had said no so bluntly. Whenever he was presented with the idea of seeing his mother, he had plenty of things he wanted to say or do. But this time, when presented with the *reality* of seeing his mother, there was a completely different response, on his part.

Before beginning our drive, I had decided on my approach to our conversation, and I pushed forward.

"Gregory, whether we see her or not is completely up to you. I think it is important that you see your mother, and you tell her what you feel, but if you don't want to go, we don't have to."

He started crying, and looked me straight in the eye, from the back seat of my truck. "I don't want to see her."

My heart broke. I pulled over, so that I could turn around and look at him face to face.

I reached out and held his hand. "I tell you what Gregory, let's drive downtown and get some dinner. You can think whether you would like to change your mind or not."

I began driving again. He was silent, seemingly for quite a while. Then he said…

"I really don't want to see her right now."

I took a deep breath. "That is your choice Gregory. But I would like to drive to where your mother is, just in case you would like to change your mind."

I didn't want to give him an easy out. I hoped he would continue to give it some thought, and perhaps would change his mind. It would have been very easy to succumb to his wishes instantly, but I had to focus.

He was quiet, as we continued to drive towards downtown Riverside.

A few minutes later he said…

"I think I would like to see my mother."

My heart stopped. I was so damned proud of him, but I needed to reassure him.

"Gregory, I am very proud of you. Let's continue to drive to where your mother is. The choice is still yours. You can change your mind, anytime you would like. But, I am very proud of you, and I think you made the right choice."

Silence. For the rest of the ride in the truck, dead silence.

Until we drove upon the city's holding facility.

"Is this the building my mommy is in?"

"Yes it is" I said. We drove up immediately adjacent to this tall, imposing building. "What do you think? Are you ready? Would you like to see her, and then go get a burger?"

"Yes I am" this brave little man said, with conviction.

We got a parking spot directly across from the Robert Presley Detention Center. The building has an ominous look. I was watching Gregory very closely, and he seemed to be doing quite well. He wasn't solemn and quiet. I remember him asking all sorts of questions, none of which related to our visit. Perhaps it was nervous chatter.

I reminded myself that if I saw anything negative, at all, I would immediately take Gregory away. I had to focus.

We walked across the street, and Gregory was skipping along while holding my hand. I remember him pulling me in a tug-of-war fashion, in multiple directions. We laughed.

This physical tug-of-war seemed quite ironic at the time.

I was experiencing an emotional tug-of-war as well…

As we walked through the main entrance, there were many people waiting inside. We had to sit and wait for quite a while, before they opened the window to allow us to sign in. During that wait, I believe it got a little more serious in his mind. There were times he was quiet. He just wanted to sit in my lap and give me hugs, and he told me multiple times how much he loved me.

But, he never gave any indication that he was under any undue stress.

We then joined the line to sign in. Gregory either stood with me, or went back over towards the seating area, where we were before. Opposed to my last visit, this seemed more like what I expected. The Sheriff's officer behind the counter just received my signature and identification, and it was very business like. Perhaps this was due to my having a previous experience. Perhaps it wasn't so surreal.

Our name was called. I remember how "eager" Gregory was to be frisked and "wanded." He smiled. He stuck his arms out like a little champ. I smiled. The Sheriff's officer who greeted him was very pleasant, and went with the mood of the moment.

He smiled as well...

As we entered the elevator, we were standing with other people. We moved up, and the other people got off on a different floor than we were headed.

I looked down at Gregory, and asked how he was doing.

He bluntly replied "good."

The doors opened, and again the room was empty. I was glad, because we got a chance to walk around a little bit, and have our own conversation. Our isolation was limited, however. Ten (or so) minutes after we got there, another mother and child entered the room, and went to the opposite side of the room.

Then I heard the doors slam open and shut. I looked up, and there was Lori, staring right at me as she walked in. I was glad she didn't change her mind. I had feared that she would refuse to see us.

She walked in, and motioned me to a chair across from the one that she wanted to sit at.

Gregory was watching this the whole time, tightly holding my hand. He looked up with a scared look on his face.

"Is that..." he asked.

"Yes, that is your mother."

He didn't recognize his mother. Another example of how much time had passed since Garrison's murder.

Gregory and I walked to where Lori was sitting. The chairs in the visitation room are very small, and round, perhaps 15 inches wide. I picked up Gregory and sat him in the chair. I kneeled onto the floor next to Gregory, on his left side. My face was at a lower elevation than Gregory's, and I was looking up at him.

I watched Gregory very closely. I kept reminding myself that if necessary I would remove Gregory instantly, without hesitation, if this was too tough on him. But he seemed to be doing ok.

He never looked up. He wouldn't look at his mother.

I picked up the phone, and chatted with Lori for a few minutes. She remarked how big he had gotten. She mentioned how good his hair cut had looked. She cried, trying to keep herself composed.

She was always so good at keeping her composure...

I set the phone down at my side, and I looked up at his face. "Would you like to say hi to your mom?" I asked.

"No thank you." Such a simple answer. So much meaning.

I have no idea how she reacted when I asked Gregory this simple question. My attention was fully on my little man.

In reality, I couldn't have cared less what she felt or thought…

Lori and I continued to talk on the phone. She said how much she missed Gregory, and she said how sorry she was. At this point, she was having a harder time keeping her composure. She covered her face with her hands often, wiping away her tears. She would look at me, but often times would avoid looking at me directly. She talked about how being away from her family was the worst thing she could imagine.

She kept saying how sorry she was…

I don't think she has ever taken full responsibility for what she did. Her words of "I am sorry that it *had* to happen" or "I don't understand why it *had* to happen" reverberate in my mind.

It *had* to happen?

And she doesn't understand why?

No personal responsibility…

As I sat there, my mind was swirling. I had to bite my lip to keep from thrashing out at her.

How dare she…

I asked Gregory if he wanted to speak with her, and again he said no.

This entire time, Gregory was looking down at his hands. I watched him as he picked at his fingernails, which seemed to be to be a common sign of his stress. I had my arm around him, and asked if he would like to leave. He said no, but he didn't want to talk to his mom. I reminded him that this visit is his choice.

A few more minutes went by, and Gregory looked down at me. He looked directly into my eyes.

"I want to say something to my mother."

My heart stopped, and I looked up at Lori. I handed Gregory the phone. He grabbed the phone with his right hand, and sitting below him on his left side, I saw him place the phone to his right ear and slowly look up towards his mother.

For the first time in over two years, Gregory spoke with his mother.

"Why did you kill my baby Garrison?"

Short. Sweet. Blunt. Matter-of-fact, forcefully, with confidence and passion.

"I don't know why, Gregory. I wish it didn't happen." Lori answered Gregory's question simply, and she looked directly into Gregory's eye. She had such a sad look on her face.

Gregory handed me the phone, looked me in the eye, and lowered his gaze back towards his hands in his lap.

He did it. He stared at his mother, and did what he had to do, but he didn't want to say anything else at that moment.

I don't remember precisely what Lori said to me on the phone. I know that I was concentrating on Gregory. I hoped he wouldn't fall apart. I really didn't want to have to "drag" him away crying or screaming – I wanted the visit to go well for him.

There was more small talk that I simply can't remember. A few more minutes passed. Then Gregory looked back down at me again.

"I would like to talk to my mom again."

I again handed him the phone. He looked up directly at her again, and with the same composure and strength…

"I am very mad at you."

I have never, ever, in my life, seen such a brave thing.

There are many heroes in this world. Firefighters, police, military, and civilians who risk their lives for others. Heroes everywhere. Heroic acts of bravery and selflessness. I have seen heroic actions personally, and everyone has heard of multiple acts of heroism.

I have never, and may not ever, see such an act of heroism and bravery again. This was such a brave little man, standing up against his mother, the woman whom he loved and trusted; the woman who not only took his little brother's life, but also removed herself as his mother, and in essence removed his older brother as well. The cascade effects of her actions were far reaching, and continue to be.

He stood up to her, and told her what he felt.

He is such a brave, strong man.

When Gregory said he was very mad at her, and I read Lori's lips. She said…

"You should be. I understand, and I am so sorry."

Perhaps she was sorry for Gregory being so mad.

I wonder if she is truly sorry for what she did…

I quickly looked back at Gregory; he handed the phone back to me, and again looked down at his hands.

A few minutes had passed, and I asked Gregory if he would like to say anything else to his mother. He said he didn't want to talk to her, so Lori and I continued to have small talk. It was mainly silence though.

Watching Gregory sit there was interesting. He continued to pick at his fingernails, but within a few minutes he began to "fidget" in his chair. He eventually got up onto his knees, a position which looked uncomfortable for him in that small chair. He was sitting on his knees, with his little butt resting on his calves, still staring downward. He slowly placed his hands on the table in front of him, and pushed his legs upwards. He leaned forward, and got taller in relation to me.

I watched him for the next couple of minutes slowly lean forward onto his arms, onto the table in front of the glass separating him from his mother. Eventually he was on his knees, resting on his forearms.

He was leaning towards his mother.

Both Lori and I noticed this. She reached her hand towards the glass, and placed her hand on the table next to the glass opposite of his hands. Gregory was exploring the table with his hands, while inching ever closer to the glass himself.

Eventually Gregory's hands made it to the glass partition. He ran his finger up onto the glass. At this point, Lori slowly moved her finger onto the glass, to where his fingers were.

This was a touching moment. No pun intended, at all.

My heart melted, somewhat. Gregory was reconnecting with his mother, to a slight extent. Here is his mother, who ripped his life apart. He loved her very much, but also had so much anger and resentment towards her.

I could only imagine what was going through his mind.

Barriers...

How interesting, how ironic, and how fitting that on the night of Garrison's murder, the shower glass door that Lori had used to pull away from me while glaring at me with her soulless eyes in such a powerfully visual manner, was now the exact same barrier between what she wanted most of all – to simply touch her son.

The image of broken bloodied shards of the shower door I had to clean up are also an interesting connection here, one that has not escaped my notice.

I spent the rest of this visit watching Lori and Gregory reconnecting just a bit. I have to give Lori credit. She tried to make him laugh. Of course, this was in her best interest as well, but I remember not caring about what she wanted at all. I wanted to see Gregory laugh a little bit, and be himself. That was my only concern at the time.

There wasn't a lot of time for them to reconnect. Most of our visit was spent getting Gregory to the point where he was comfortable. The buzzer went off, and we were told that the visit was over.

As we were getting ready to leave, Lori asked if I could bring him back again. She thanked me multiple times for coming. She was sincere.

Gregory said good bye to his mother. It was a very simple moment, with no excruciating emotional outbursts. Gregory did what he had to do, he did what he wanted to do, and he was ready to leave. I asked if he was hungry, and he said yes. I remember turning around, as the elevator door opened up. Lori looked me in the eye, and whispered "thank you" to me. I nodded, and smiled.

Then the elevator door closed. I finally breathed.

I remember walking outside with Gregory. Nice cool evening fresh air. It was dark, and the street was lit up with lots of lights. It was such a refreshing walk to my truck. Gregory was in a very good mood, and wouldn't stop talking. He was talking about a lot of things, most of which I can't remember, but I do remember that he didn't talk much about his mother. His mind was now elsewhere.

Then this brave little man and I got a cheeseburger. I do believe it was the best cheeseburger of my entire life. I don't remember anything that was said. I remember the laughter and giggles.

And that was it.

I am so glad that I listened to his counselor. I am so glad that I listened to the other people who encouraged me to do this. I am so glad that I didn't tell anyone else what I was thinking. I am so glad that I overcame my fears, my inhibitions, and my protectionism. This was so important, and it wasn't about me. This was all about Gregory, and he was amazing.

I think my focusing on his best interests, against everything that I felt to my core, was one of the best decisions I have ever made.

Perhaps this is good advice for anyone, under similar circumstances.

I took Gregory to see his mother, one last time. Her sentencing hearing was postponed, so I had a little more time. The second visit was light-hearted, and Gregory got to tell his mother all about his life. He talked all about his friends, his baseball, his teachers, his interests. They talked a lot, and kept it very superficial. This visit was more about his reconnecting with his mother a little.

I am glad I allowed Gregory to see his mother again, that one last time. I thought it may be the last time he sees her. That is up to him. But at least until he is 18 years old, I will do what I feel is in his best interest. If it is in Gregory's best interest, I will take him to see her at some point. There are no plans to continue fostering a relationship with her.

He hasn't asked to see her since that second visit.

I would like to conclude this section with a few words of thanks to the Riverside Sheriff's Department, who are in charge of the holding facility where Lori was held for over two years.

I made three visits to Lori within those few weeks. The first visit was to ascertain whether Gregory would (or should) be brought there. The second visit was Gregory's first confrontation with his mother. The third visit was, in my opinion, a final "good bye" visit between Gregory and his mother.

What I am about to say, I do not know for a fact. These are just my feelings, based on my impressions. So please bear with me.

On my first visit, when I was checking in, (as I stated earlier) it seemed as if the officer who was present when I signed in recognized who I was immediately, when I stated who I was going to visit. Not that he recognized me personally, but based on the fact that he knew who Lori was. Having her husband making a visit must have been surprising, perhaps. But I did feel as if our eyes met in a certain moment of "recognition," in the seriousness and significance of the moment. I doubt that my visit was anticipated (who on earth would visit the murderer of his child?).

There were a lot of people waiting to see inmates. The waiting period was excruciating. Cramped, crowded, loud, and smelly. But, when I got up to the visiting area, it was empty. Was this coincidence? When I was standing in this large room, by myself, for seemingly an eternity, it was awfully quiet. I fully expected other visitors to come through the elevator door at anytime. I expected to see other inmates.

None of this happened.

My initial visit with Lori should have taken about 45. Granted, there was some time where I was alone prior to our meeting, but it sure seemed as if it was a lot longer than was officially allowed.

I was definitely given alone time with her, with no other inmates or visitors present, ever.

I am fully aware that our conversation was monitored. I am fully aware that our conversation was video-taped. I expected this, prior to walking into that room. It seemed reasonable.

What I didn't expect was to be given complete privacy, for such a long period of time. This may, or may not, have happened intentionally. But it is my humble opinion that the Riverside

Sheriff's Department realized the significance of this visit, and gave me enough space to allow me to do what I had to do.

Like I said, these are my thoughts. Chances are the visit didn't last as long as I thought. Chances are it was just pure chance that we were alone for such a long time. Chances are the Sheriff at the counter, when I checked in, hadn't a clue who I was.

However, if I am correct, thank you so much, to everyone involved. You helped give me strength to do what I had to do, and I am forever grateful.

My Focus: The Victim's Impact Statement

I did not want to do this. I was convinced that it would serve no benefit, that it would have no value. As the time approached, and it became evident to everyone that I was considering not providing a statement, the prosecutor Will Robinson took a few minutes to speak with me. He asked why I was considering not making a statement. He suggested that if I wanted to write something, but didn't feel comfortable enough to read it personally in court, that it could be read for me, to be placed onto the official court record. He emphasized that it was more to do with the "value" of making the statement for the record.

What words could I possibly say to illustrate the "impact" this murder had on me and my family? I didn't want to use this as an opportunity to get in front of the judge to bitch and moan about my pain. I wanted nothing to do with that.

His next words in fact convinced me to deliver the impact statement, and I would hope others could take this advice as well.

"If Lori was up for parole tomorrow, and the parole board held a hearing for her release, would you testify why she should not be released?"

Such a simple question for this brilliant man to ask.

"Of course I would" I numbly responded.

"Why?" he asked.

"Because I fear for Gregory's safety, and I can't trust that she wouldn't do this again."

I thought to myself *"duh, I am not that stupid."*

"What if you die tonight? How would the parole board know exactly what your thoughts are tomorrow?"

Silence.

Pure moments of intellectual realization can cause deafening silence.

I had spent five or six days being interrogated on the witness stand. I had spent five or six days in front of the judge, being admonished for certain answers, being directed to stick to the facts of the case only, not being allowed to express anything about my feelings or emotions, being kept from seeing other witnesses or testimony for weeks on end – I had been kept "locked up" for quite a while through the entire process.

The reality is that if I had died, no one would know how I felt. What if I died? What if Lori indeed got out of prison?

So I agreed to write the impact statement. I declined the offer to have it read for me. If I were going to do this, I would do this on my terms.

I walked into the courtroom, and made the long walk towards the podium. I had written the impact statement, in the form of outline notes. Much of what I said was extemporaneous, with my notes there to help guide me through what I had to say.

This is my impact statement, written from my memory, based on my notes which I had typed (and saved) on my computer. It may not be verbatim to what I stated in court (I have never gotten a transcript). However, it is very close, and for illustrative purposes, this works just fine.

Madame Judge,

First of all I would like to offer my profound thanks to the court for this opportunity. I would also like to offer my sincere thanks to the Riverside Police Department for their professionalism in my time of need. I would like to thank the Deputy Public Defender Gail O'Rane, whose defense of my wife was admirable, and difficult, given the facts of the case. I would like to thank Deputy District Attorney Will Robinson for his patience, his professionalism, and for his encouragement. I would also like to thank Kym Conover and the Riverside County District Attorney's Office Division of Victim Services for everything that they have done for me and my family. I couldn't have imagined getting through this without their support and encouragement. I would also like to thank the RCCD Early Childhood Studies Program, countless friends, family and colleagues for their incredible support of me and my family.

What is a Victims Impact Statement? How can you summarize, in a few words, the impact such a tragedy has on a family? I have decided to summarize the impact what is known, and what is unknown.

The impact of the known – the loss of Garrison. I lost my infant son Garrison. A beautiful child was murdered, and taken from those who love him.

The impact of the known – the impact to Nick. His mother kept him home the day of the murder, as a full witness in the event. His discovery of Garrison's body, and sitting there in the house all day virtually as a prisoner. His mother telling him to "trust me." Nick's refusal to seek professional help. Nick's total lack of discipline, and respect for those who surround him. He steals, he lies, he manipulates, and he uses drugs. Lori's loss in Nick's life is a vacuum to Nick's focus and discipline.

The impact of the known – the impact to Gregory. In that fateful day, Gregory lost his mother, and his best friend Garrison. Gregory also lost his brother Nick as a major and integral part of his life. In the 774 days since Garrison's murder, he has gotten to see Nick on 29 separate days, which is 3.7% of his life.

The impact of the known – the cascade effects. The events of this murder, and the subsequent time thereafter, has impacted close family, friends, and the community. These effects are far too reaching for me to comment, on any reasonable level.

The impact of the known – Lori's state of mind. Lori was found criminally sane. I have learned through this process that criminal sanity is independent of medical insanity. She is currently psychotic and delusional, and not receiving any form of treatment.

The impact of the unknown – the loss of Garrison. His innocent laughter, his smiles, his tears, and his value to many peoples' lives and society will never be known.

The impact of the unknown – had Gregory been home. Lori assumed that Gregory would be home with Garrison the day of the murder. She was surprised to find Gregory gone in the morning when she woke up. She had full intent to murder Gregory, along with Garrison. It was pure chance, and by accident, that I took Gregory to day care, which saved his life.

The impact of the unknown – Nick's future. How will Lori's use of the words "trust me" impact his relationships? Lori was a guiding force, and very instrumental in Nick's life. How can you predict the loss of Lori as a positive influence, and the adversely negative impacts on his life? I fear for Nick's future – other than the loss of Garrison, the downward spiral of Nick's life is the single biggest tragedy of Garrison's murder.

The impact of the unknown – Gregory's future. Immediately after the murder, I sought the help of professional child therapists, with specific training in traumatic events. My immediate focus for Gregory: His respect, trust and self-confidence in himself. His respect and trust of a woman. His growth into a good man, and a good human. As it turns out, Gregory may be better off right now. He has benefited from not being immersed and surrounded in a home atmosphere of angst, anger, and rage. Gregory is well-adjusted, happy, and blossomed as a person. Gregory has amazing strength and self-confidence. He hadn't seen Lori for two years (which is 40% of his life). He was given the choice to see Lori this week, and with a lot of apprehension, he decided to see her. His first words to his mother: "Why did you kill my baby Garrison?" and "I am mad at you." Seeing this little man, stare at his mother, and say those words, may have been the bravest event that I have ever witnessed. After this, he was able to laugh with his mother, and enjoy his visit. He was very happy that he went, and so I was I. Gregory's future looks bright. Gregory's happiness, confidence, and success are the primary reason for my being.

The Impact of the unknown - Lori's State of Mind. Prior to the murder, had you asked me, there would have been a 0% chance that she would ever hurt any of her children. You can never, on any intellectual level, with confidence, say that she is incapable of hurting anyone, ever again. Lori has not, and is not, receiving professional and medical treatment for her psychosis. Lori has never taken personal responsibility for her actions. She has stated that she is a "puppet of God" and she has no free will or independent actions or thoughts. She believes that all of her actions are pre-destined and pre-ordained. Because of Lori's reality, Lori cannot ever be trusted to be put in any position where she could potentially harm anyone else, ever again.

How can I summarize "impact" in a simple statement? How do I put into words the far-reaching effect this has had up to this point, and the potential effect far into the future? I didn't come here to bitch and moan.

But when it comes to Lori Burchett's sentencing, for the heinous, cold-blooded, methodical, brutal, murder of MY beautiful 17 month-old Garrison Lee Burchett on February 23, 2009 – Lori, Fuck You.

That was it.

The cumulative weight of the day, of the trial, of her sentence, of the potential of her getting out of jail, of the murder, of my finding Garrison's body, of the pain I had witnessed and experienced, of my profound loss and agony suddenly hit me like a tidal wave. Two years of pain and agony, sitting behind a giant dam, suddenly caused the greatest flood of emotion I could possibly imagine.

I walked out of the courtroom instantly, and went into the hallway. I broke down crying, and I shook violently. My body was covered in sweat. Kym Conover sat next to me, trying to help me calm down. After a few moments, we walked back into the courtroom just in time for her sentence to be read.

Lori was sentenced to 25 years to life, with time served.

Prior to my re-entering the courtroom, evidently the Judge asked defense counsel to look into Nick's welfare, and proposed getting him help.

My focus culminated that day.

Reading that impact statement for the record, speaking slowly and with purpose, was one of the most difficult things I have ever had to do. Not quite as bad as walking down that hallway, knowing full well that I would discover something terribly wrong. That night, I was numb, and I wasn't in control. This statement was all on my shoulders.

Because of the heinous nature of this crime my wife committed, ritualistically murdering our 17 month old son, Garrison, a powerful statement had to be made. I stepped up and delivered it with everything that I had to give, and with all of the strength that I could muster.

I did it.

My focus was so instrumental. Focus kept me alive, focus kept me strong, and focus kept me going when I didn't think I had anything else to give. Focus is what I believe helped me get through the most difficult times of my life. I still struggle to find focus in my daily life, but I appreciate how focus helped me.

In a letter Lori wrote me from prison later, she expressed shock and disappointment at what I said. She said that I had been so supportive of her during our visits. She said that my words in court really hurt.

She confuses my biting my lip, and my not jumping down her throat, as "support" of her. She confuses my focus and strength, for the sake of Gregory, as support for her. She confuses my being very articulate in her presence, in the words of everything that I said to her, as support of her.

She has no idea of how much anger I truly have…

Focus.

Such a simple word.

Such a difficult thing in life.

To take time, be patient, breathe, and focus.

Chapter 5:
Cranial Rectal Insertion

The vision of an ostrich sticking its head in the sand is often synonymous with being ignorant of a situation, and not seeing what is so obvious, by choosing not to be aware. The term "pull your head out of your ass" is more personal to most people, and generally can elicit a laughing response or two. I prefer another term which I call "cranial-rectal insertion" (CRI) which is a humorous visual that I have relied upon for many years. I like to think I actually thought of it, but chances are I heard it somewhere else. This vision of a person being severely contorted in a way which makes it impossible for them to see anything, to me at least, seems funny. Of course, often in my life I use sarcasm to make a point, at least to myself.

When I think of what happened to Garrison, of all of the "links" in the chain which led to this disaster, and of all of the things that I missed, it is very evident that I suffered from my so-called "cranial-rectal insertion" in a most troubling way. I go through my mind; I recall conversations, and I think about the things that I had seen and heard. I guess it is natural to look at life through the prism of hindsight and its "20/20 vision," and as is often said, it is so much clearer after-the-fact.

I tried to explain earlier that it seemed like my life was a puzzle, and as pieces were being placed together the totality of the story became more evident. However, this story didn't really make sense, until that last piece was put into place. That piece was my discovering Garrison's lifeless body.

Those specific pieces, the missing links or warning signs that I had missed, the examples of rage, anger, and Lori's downward psychological spiral are what I was ignorant to.

I suffered from "cranial-rectal insertion" in the most profound, devastating, and humbling way.

Had I not been so ignorant, had I not been so emotionally blindly biased, had I not been living in fear and walking on egg shells, and had I not been so utterly forgiving and eternally optimistic, I may not have missed something that was fundamentally important. These "links" which I have mentioned – her anger, her controlling nature, her neuroticism, and her Godly conversations are all so important, to how I see my life now, and how (in retrospect) my life was then. I cannot minimize their importance. They directly impacted my "themes" of living in fear, and resulted in my focus.

All it would have taken is for me to catch *one* of these signs, just one of the missing links. Just one piece out of a thousand would have taken my life journey in a completely different path, and quite possibly Garrison's murder could have been avoided.

How easy does that sound?

I would fully expect any reader of this book to look at my words, and often say *"what the…."* and question how "obvious" she was "insane," and that she was going to do something terribly wrong.

However, please remember you are reading this, and judging what had happened, from the perspective of *knowing* what has happened – not what could be.

I was trying to keep my family together, I was trying desperately to help my wife, and I was trying to understand. I was just like any other person, wrapped up in the situation of life, swimming in all of life's emotions. I may have been trying to think rationally, and I may have been unable to do so. I was also emotionally exhausted.

I live every day of my life regretting the things that I missed. I blame myself every day for Garrison's murder, and I hate living life like this. The culmination of everything that Lori did to our lives, everything that Lori did to each of us, and everything that I feel that I missed is so painful inside. The blame that I rest upon my shoulders is my burden, because of my "missing" something along the way.

Someday, hopefully, I can move past this. It was Lori's fault, and on most reasonable levels, I couldn't have been expected to stop what would have inevitably happened.

Intellectually I know that it was her fault. Emotionally, I blame myself.

So here I am, admitting that I had my head shoved so far up my large intestine that I was completely blind, deaf, and unaware of the world around me.

Hopefully, somehow, this will help someone "pull their head out." Hopefully this can help someone save a life, and hopefully this will help someone not live their life in regret.

The Chain Revealed

When trying to organize my thoughts in describing what I missed, I think that following up with my "themes" seemed best. Perhaps this is just how my mind works, and I hope that it makes sense to the reader as well. In each of these, there will be a few illustrative examples to help make the bigger point with perspective, many of which I have eluded to previously. I sincerely believe that one of the biggest mistakes that I made is not realizing how much I was being manipulated by Lori. She used my emotional weaknesses (i.e. living in fear, my eternal optimism) in a very manipulative manner, which led me to either make poor choices, or choose not to make the right choice (in-and-of-itself a choice).

Lori's downward psychological spiral was a miserable thing to be a part of. It seemed that the themes were all interconnected - by her psychosis. Her anger may have been an extension of her desire to be in control. Her neuroticism may have been an extension of this control (or lack thereof), which further led to her Godly conversations. It was all interconnected by innumerable fibers in the total fabric of life.

Not knowing the extent of her changing psychosis was one thing, but what I have experienced, and what I believe I should have seen, is another. I have multiple examples which *could* have led *someone else*, someone far more intelligent than I, who actually knew what signs to look for, that would seriously cause her mindset, her reality, and her sanity, to be in question. Perhaps someone not caught up in the moment, perhaps someone not embroiled in the dizzying reality, and perhaps someone not so emotionally involved could be *that* intelligent.

In the immortal words of the great Neil Peart of RUSH, "if you choose not to decide, you still have made a choice…"

What does that mean? Had I been more forceful in getting her some help, perhaps someone else could have seen this…

I should have dialed 911 on the day which that she damaged the car. I chose not to, perhaps because I didn't realize I needed to make that choice. I don't remember the thought crossing my mind at all.

But the choices we make, to either do something, or not do anything, all add up after a while…

Psychological Spin Control

Lori was always angry. Perhaps you have gathered this point by now. She, self-admittedly, had a hard time controlling her anger, and her rage. It manifested itself on multiple occasions, and quite often she reacted in very inappropriate ways.

I believe that Lori struggled. I believe that she recognized that she had problems, and I believe that she sincerely wanted to find inner peace. Her anger, and her need for control, may have been a manifestation of this struggle. Perhaps, throughout her life, she kept "it" together, barely, on the surface. Perhaps, from a casual observer, she was calm and collected, with moments that were absolutely inappropriate.

Perhaps, she was always a mess inside, and perhaps she just lost her ability to keep it under control. Perhaps, her "control" was like walking on thin ice, with a fragile sliver of her conscious control, suspended upon the deep liquid "reality" underneath.

Lori began, quite noticeably, to change her behavior after Garrison was born. As I have discussed earlier, she became overprotective of him, and refused to take him to child care. Her thought processes, as illustrated in our discussions with each other, and "our" decisions, became quite interesting, to say the least. She began exploring the spiritual and psychological side of her life. Not that this is inherently wrong, but I believe that her thought process during this time became distorted.

A little bit of knowledge can be a very dangerous thing...

Self-Diagnosis Revisited

Lori began to notice small changes in herself, and began to ask serious questions about herself. I think that initially this "introspection" was good, much of which I fully supported, but there are many examples of how this led to neurotic behavior.

As I have mentioned, she diagnosed herself as bi-polar. She did this by doing extensive research on the web, with (in my opinion) a neurotic enthusiasm. As with many people, once they begin to learn about something, and they find information which seems to agree with their *a priori* ideas or assumptions, they naturally "grab" for it. Unfortunately, most of what is on the web is not fact-based, and is subject to tremendous interpretation. And how sad, looking at a lot of information, "deleting" most of it in your head, and only "seeing" what you *want* to see.

Most people, quite naturally, gravitate towards any information that suits their pre-conceived notions or opinions.

In this case, she saw some aspects of bi-polar disorder that she related to, but I also think she missed many of the other clinical diagnostic signs that didn't reflect her mindset.

That being said, once she "realized" exactly what she "believed" and had "decided" what was causing her so much trouble, she then began telling her close friends and family members that "they" were also bi-polar.

Because she now "knew" what she was talking about, she was now an "authority" and would bluntly tell others their woes. I can think of at least five other people for whom she made this diagnosis, starkly informing them of this fact over the phone. She hurt these people by saying these words.

The news media jumped all over the "fact" that Lori was bi-polar, and this was factually incorrect. She never received a formal diagnosis, although she was beginning to get some help (albeit reluctantly).

This "fact" of her diagnosis came from a false rumor. This was made from an incorrect statement, made to the media, by Lori's Uncle. This was the same person who had lived in my house immediately following the murder and who stole from me. Quite simply, he was relishing his time in the limelight, desperately looking for financial gain from this tragedy, and made many statements that were inflammatory and factually incorrect.

I give Lori some credit - She did seek out professional help. She spoke to them. But that was the extent of what happened. She would *begin* asking for help, but would not "like" what she heard, and therefore didn't want to move forward. It is as if she was looking for the "path of least resistance" in her life, and only wanted to hear the answers she was seeking.

As always, she was in "control" of everything in her life, including her own diagnosis. Official diagnosis be damned... Official treatments be damned...

Again, to my knowledge, she was never officially diagnosed as bi-polar, or with any other psychological affliction. It is possible that all of these professionals had a "gut feeling" or opinion of her, but I don't think that there was enough time to adequately diagnose her. The fact that she was never clinically diagnosed was a major factor in her trial, when trying to ascertain whether she was criminally insane or not.

I have indeed discovered that there is a distinct difference between medical insanity, and criminal insanity, and this took a long time for me to come to its realization.

When she did begin to see someone, and they began her on temporary medical therapy as part of their initial diagnosis and treatment, she didn't like the side-effects. Some of these side-effects were legitimate; one medication in particular actually affected Garrison through her breast milk. In this particular case, he became lethargic for a day (or so). We immediately spoke with her physician, and decided to cease using that medication. Other side-effects were just "possibilities" which were often only known to her from her "extensive" research on the web. She would adamantly refuse treatment based on the perceived potential side effects, and based on the fact that she didn't agree with what she was being told.

Again, through her extensive (i.e. neurotic) research on the web, she became an "expert" on this subject, as well as all potential diagnostic and treatment options. This is why she would adamantly disagree with her doctors. She eventually decided that she didn't trust conventional medicine. She argued with enthusiastic emphasis that they just wanted to make money, and turn her into a zombie with medicines.

She became convinced that she could self-treat herself. Why not? She had done her own diagnosis...

Self-Treatment Revisited

Her self-treatment followed several primary areas of emphasis. As I have mentioned, Lori wanted to become healthier physically, and as part of this, began attending yoga classes. She wanted to get stronger, and lose the weight she gained while being pregnant with Garrison, and began focusing her attentions to her health, her diet, and natural/herbal supplements.

Lori wanted to become healthier, she wanted to become more relaxed, and less angry or stressed. Without hesitation, I wanted this for her as well. I fully supported her in finding her inner peace.

Anger was the most pressing issue, from both of our perspectives. Lori would wake up, and she would be extremely angry. She could never explain "why" she was angry, but she knew she was. Over time, I became very good at recognizing instantly if this would be a "good day," or a "bad day" depending on her mood. I was very sensitive to these differing "moods" in her life. I found myself always gauging her "temperature" and responding to her.

These changes in her mood were some of her main concerns, and her preferred method of self-treatment was marijuana. She honestly felt that with marijuana, she could keep her anger at bay, and this opinion was "validated" when she got a prescription for medical marijuana. She generally would go outside to "treat" herself, but amazingly she would sometimes just simply walk from our bedroom, walk straight into the kitchen, and stand under the vent above the stove to allow the smoke to escape.

Sadly, from my perspective, she was often much happier when she was high. She was much more pleasant to be around. Unfortunately (or fortunately), she also fully realized this fact.

Our yoga experiences were quite different. I enjoyed yoga, going to classes as often as I could. It was relaxing for me, very good from a physical standpoint, and extremely beneficial for my lower back which I injured when I was 17 years old.

But, what started as an enjoyable outlet for exercise for Lori, became much more important than that to her. She began to relish her time away from the family, needing the alone time. This focus on her alone time became quite important, and would actually cause stress when she didn't get that alone time. If, for example, she would miss a class due to a conflict with my scheduling, she would focus her rage towards me.

As her yoga experience became a bigger part of her daily activities, she also began to explore more personal, and spiritual, aspects of herself.

I have tried very hard not to blame yoga, in any way, for her downward spiral. But it is evident that her experiences with yoga did at least open some doors, in many aspects, to her proclaimed self-realization and introspection. It would be ignorant of me to deny that her emotional state spiraling downward was not intimately involved with her yoga experience.

Her involvement with yoga also became a focus in the investigations immediately following Garrison's death. There was a large amount of time and energy investigating the extent to which the people involved with yoga were involved with her life prior to Garrison's murder. Thankfully, the investigations found no direct relationships. It would have saddened me greatly if I discovered that those wonderful people were directly involved, assuming that their private discussions with Lori didn't contribute to the centrifugal force of my life as it was spinning out of control.

Perhaps, as I write this, my opinion has changed somewhat. The discovery of *The Dark Night of the Soul*, and the delayed realization that this book was given to her by *someone* at the yoga studio, has left a bitter taste in my mouth. Perhaps this book was a "blip" on her radar, and didn't affect what was happening. Perhaps it was a significant part of what happened. I guess I don't know that answer, so therefore I am unable to fully process this – as of yet.

It was during Lori's time of becoming more enthralled with yoga that she experienced "the awakening" during a yoga session. It was also at this time that she began discussing the possibility of traveling to India. I re-emphasize these two points of interest, only to offer perspective as to the timing of these events.

This "awakening" was a monumentally emotional experience for her. She shared with me some of what she felt, but I don't think that she imparted upon me the true depth of her experience. Her desire to substantially change her life, to look for something that was inside of her, to travel and meet others who may help her discover who she actually was, became such a vital motivational force in her life.

In addition to yoga and her marijuana use, another area of self-treatment was in her use of natural, or herbal, medications. I have already discussed this to some extent, illustrating examples like kombucha, the fermented tea.

This is also where I believe that I missed some of the signs. In retrospect, Lori's focus on her health, actually became unhealthy. She became neurotic about her health, she made unreasonable and irrational decisions, and she began spending an excessive amount of money on her health.

I was desperate, and at times I was not thinking rationally. Lori spent literally thousands of dollars a month on her supplements. She had dramatically increased spending, immediately after impulsively quitting her job. This added so much stress into my life, and I felt that I had to continue to purchase these products for her. Her anger, her angst, her diminished perspectives all contributed to my reactions to her, and to my emotional reality making me blind to the reality of my life.

I guess I just wanted her happy, at any cost...

Our local health food store was very happy to see us walk through the doors.

I remember a somewhat funny moment. Less than a month before Garrison died, two of my dear friends came over for a visit. When they walked into the kitchen, they saw jars of liquid with a film-like fungus growing on top sitting on the counters. It was the kombucha I was growing for Lori. The look on my friend's face, when we began explaining what we were attempting to do, was that of interest, disgust, and disbelief. I thought it was quite funny.

But it was also sad – I wonder what they were thinking about me at that moment. I have never asked them that. Perhaps I should.

Planning for the Future

I keep coming back to the fact that no matter how bad my swirl of emotion was, no matter how bad Lori acted, and that no matter how painful these experiences may have been, I always retained a sense of optimism.

Lori seemed to recognize that she had problems. Lori seemed to realize that she needed to address these problems, although now it seems that she didn't go about it in the right way. Lori seemed to be telling me about her experiences, although now it seems that she kept much from me.

But we always discussed the future. Lots of different discussions, but those discussions were there. Too many discussions, too many ideas, and too many swirling moments in time to remember.

Moving to India. Moving to another state. Retiring. Raising our children. Finding inner peace. Lots of thoughts about the future.

Her career was also always spoken through a prism of optimism.

Her short-term goals included slowly completing her certificate in ESL studies (English as a Second Language), and pursue a professorship.

Lori quitting her job suddenly changed the timing of this, but not the ultimate goal. Optimistically speaking, we thought that this would give her a chance to finish her ESL studies, and move forward towards her new career. We were going to take a hit financially, but I thought it would be short-term. Perhaps it was because we had made plans for Lori to change careers that made it easier for her to quit.

So we planned on spending the rest 2008 optimistically working towards the future. She spent that year finishing her certificate, and she even began applying for teaching positions. Optimistically, we had hoped she would get a teaching position as quickly as possible.

This optimism continued, even in the swirl of our emotional turmoil. It was the Friday prior to Garrison's death that we opened a bottle of wine, celebrating her getting the application packet into Riverside City College. We had a good feeling that she would get hired.

What a dichotomy of emotion and situational reality…

God's Plan or Psychosis?

I have previously mentioned that Lori heard God's voice. He was speaking to her. She would see His messages when she looked at an object, she would hear His voice come through the car stereo.

She has said it was God's will that Garrison be sent to heaven. She continues to say that she doesn't understand "why it *had* to happen" and that she wishes that it "didn't *have* to happen," all the while not ever taking responsibility for what did to make "it" happen; she murdered our son.

After Garrison's death, one of the discoveries that the investigative detectives discovered on our computer was her web browsing history. There was one website, in particular, which seemed to have a tremendous impact on her thinking. I believe that this website, in addition to the *Dark Night of the Soul*, may have been her basis of our conversations concerning the "scroll," the infinity sign, and ego that I previously discussed.

I would really like to see this scroll again. Perhaps someday I will gather the courage to ask the D.A.'s office if this is a possibility. The only time I did see it, it was such a torrent of emotion, a mind-numbing conversation, and there is so much that I can't recall.

I do remember Lori's elation, her anger, her sadness, and her sickening reality of my not "understanding" of what she felt. The look on her face, as she grabbed the scroll and clutching it to her chest, will be forever burned into my memory.

It was as if I had the emotional wind knocked out of me. I was breathless, and I was numb. I wasn't "coping" with what was happening.

Lori came to believe that the end of the world was coming. There would be a "safe haven" in Utah, and that she wanted to go there. This is one of the aspects of her thinking that she kept secret from me. I went to this particular website, and what I saw disgusted me, and made my stomach sick. Almost everything that she was saying to me came from that website. And it has become evident that the brutal way in which Garrison was murdered – you could easily say sacrificed – was ritualistic in nature, and had tremendous religious meaning. This website also professed the virtue of mummification ceremonies, and evidently this was discussed during her trial.

The weekend prior to Garrison passing, she told me that she drove our car into a telephone pole, because God told her to do so. I have mentioned this previously, but this is of vital importance. I should have taken the keys away from her. There was physical damage on that car (even if she didn't hit a telephone pole). I should have told Lori that she would never drive again, especially with anyone else in the car. This was more than her merely having strange thoughts – this was Lori choosing to use the car as a weapon. Lori's crazed ranting and raving, trying to explain to me that she was "directed" by God, and in her staunch belief that she did the right thing.

I was lost. I was stupid. I was so fucking ignorant. I missed that link.

I should have called 911 that day. Often I wonder if during her "72 hour lockdown" she would have been able to put on an act to convince everyone she was ok, or indeed succumb to her reality in their presence.

Had she been released immediately after that 72 hours with no recommendation for treatment, my life would have been quite miserable. I know she would have left me immediately with my two sons.

I was living in fear of what I may lose. I was blinded by my optimism, and I was blinded by my love. My eternal optimism led to my blind love. I never, ever, in a million years, would have thought that Lori was capable of hurting her children. I believe that I thought she would shave her head, move to India, and discover herself.

Never hurt her kids…

Ever hurt her kids…

But this car was a weapon, one which held great power, being controlled by a woman who had no control. God directed her to drive. God told her how to drive.

This car was a weapon, wielded by a disturbed person.

Let your friend drive drunk? Absolutely not – take the keys from him, even at the risk of your friendship.

Let a deranged person drive a car, when God is telling her to drive it into a telephone pole just to test her faith? Of course, I didn't know this before-hand.

I was so blind...

Had I recognized this link, had I taken her keys away that day, and had I told someone, something in the path of my life might have been different. I am convinced that somehow Garrison would be alive – or at least not been killed on that specific day. Weak links can destroy a strong chain. When this realization hit me, I was crippled inside.

I came to this realization at an odd-time. It was during my testimony in trial, and during cross-examination, when defense counsel questioned my actions during this point, and why I hadn't taken more steps to get her help, attempting to squarely place as much blame as possible onto my shoulders. This is when this realization hit me, and I was crippled inside emotionally.

I still am...

Many people, both personally and professionally, will advise me that there are many aspects of this line of thought where I am flawed, and that there was little I could have done. Thank you for trying to make me feel better about myself, but that was a huge link. A huge link that I missed. A very small piece of a very large puzzle that directly led to his murder.

And I missed it...

How ironic. I have thought about this quandary quite a lot, and finally came to a realization that this in fact was something that I missed. Put blame, whatever the amount, upon my shoulders. Now I have more reason to eternally beat myself up.

Add to that, the memories of listening to the closing statements made by her defense counsel during the sanity phase of her trial. Lori reached out to Greg. He didn't help. No one helped her. Fantastic. What a brilliant observation. Lay as much blame as possible onto my shoulders, in order to bolster her insanity. Thank you very much. I don't blame the defense counsel for doing their job, however.

As if I weren't beating myself up already. Now the defense council claims that Garrison's murder was because I didn't see the signs...

By the way, to those who think this is part of God's plan – if I was destined to live my life, through all of my turmoil, good times, tough times, good choices, and poor choices, to have an off-chance meeting with a woman, in order to get married, get pregnant with Gregory, buy a home, live a life, in order to have another off chance of one sperm amongst hundreds of billions, to randomly fertilize a specific egg in one of two oviducts, having a perfect pregnancy and normal fetal development, in order to give birth to a second beautiful son, watching this beautiful small being become a "person" in front of my eyes - in order for him to be murdered by his own mother – If this is part of His plan, then He and I will have a discussion someday.

I know that "it's part of His plan" is actually solace for the person saying it, but if my life was destined to witness my wife's soulless eyes after discovering my son Garrison's lifeless body, and the ripple-effect aftermath of that murder at the hands of his own mother, I seriously question that plan. On any intellectual level, you must question this "predestination."

Machination

One of the most troubling areas of my life that I came to realize only after Garrison's murder, was how Lori controlled and manipulated me, in order to get what she really wanted. I believe that this overt manipulation, in its entire context, was a driving force behind Lori's being found *criminally sane* during the sanity phase of her trial. Because she was so articulate, so manipulative, and so thoughtful in her actions and planning, she had mental faculties which argued for her being criminally liable for her actions, and against her "insanity."

During the sentencing hearing, the presiding judge actually admonished Lori for her attempting to manipulate the court as well. I was astonished – I didn't know what had happened, in order for this judge to say that. I wondered how Lori could have attempted this manipulation.

I guess it wasn't just me…

Had someone told me that she had also been manipulating me as well, I would have had a hard time grasping it. Who wouldn't? It wasn't until I read her words later, that this reality occurred to me, in its entirety.

Lori held great power over me, emotionally. She wielded this power, at her whim, to get what she wanted. In hindsight, I feel as if I was tugged in multiple ways, however I also believe that her manipulation wasn't "complete" and there were some aspects of her attempted manipulation in which she failed. Maybe this is why her need for control turned to neuroticism.

Perhaps I was stronger than I give myself credit for.

Unfortunately, from her perspective, my agreeing to many of her wishes was evidence (to her) of my weaknesses, and gave her a false impression that she could get away with anything.

This false impression fueled her false bravado...

In fact, in some respects, she continues to attempt to manipulate me. She has written that she wants to come home, and build our family again. She has said that she wants to be a part of Gregory's life. She is convinced that she will be released on appeal, and that she wants to come "home." She has said that she doesn't know "why" it "had" to happen, and wishes that "it" didn't "have" to happen.

The mind is a terrible thing...

In Her Own Words

My spending time going through our computer illustrated how little I knew what was actually going on in Lori's mind. This was a tough realization on my part, and it shed light on what she was actually going through, and how I couldn't have even comprehended what she was going through no matter how hard I had tried.

Reading through her words, I can't help but be reminded of those conversations that we had. It's hard to put them into perspective, much less try to describe them here. These conversations were "all over" the place, and had so many topics, had so many perspectives, and on many levels, were so difficult to grasp.

During the trial, her writings on the computer were included as part of the investigation, and in determining the context of her mindset. I guess to some extent I am thankful that she was more open and honest with her fingers typing on the computer, than she ever was in any of her discussions with me. I have no idea why, except perhaps her lack of respect and trust in who I was, and my place in her life. Perhaps she was truly scared to share her honest thoughts, with anyone.

Detectives asked me what these files referred to. Defense investigators wanted to know my interpretation. I tried to help them, but in reality I didn't know. When she spoke to me, often these words were said – but it was all so confusing.

I don't know whether including these words is a good thing, or not. There are arguments for and against their inclusion. But, I hope that they can help shed some light, especially when read by qualified people, who may be able to use this section in its context, and be able to help others.

I placed these files in chronological order. I have also not edited these in any way, other than to italicize the words.

These are her written words.

As I found these words, and as I began to read them, I was furious. As I continued reading these words, the night she clutched the scroll in her arms, with rage in her face yelling at how I would never understand, began to make sense.

I saw her face, and I lived that confusion, all over again.

Perhaps this section will help others see this woman on her downward journey. Perhaps reading this section will help others experience what it was like in that kitchen, watching someone I loved ramble in an incoherent way.

Perhaps reading this section will give the reader context and perspective of my centrifugal force, and how I saw my life spinning out of control.

Perhaps reading this section will allow the reader to imagine standing in that kitchen…

And not knowing what to do.

"LORI'S LIST" (August 14, 2008)

T- Minus 193 days until Garrison's Murder. We had just vacated our home and moved.

I understand now why you go. I would go too, if I could.

I think of you. No, I don't think.

I feel.

I feel you so strongly. I know that you are thinking of me, too, wherever you are, thinking these same thoughts, sort of. Your version of these thoughts. These feelings that lead to these thoughts. There I go, off, right?

You taught me presence. You tried to. I tried very hard to follow. You have no idea the effort I put forth to be as commonly noble as I could be. Thank you for that lesson. I needed it. You know I did.

And perhaps I taught you to, what? Not to connect, or maybe to only connect. I don't know. I feel so many questions without words about it, it which seems to have a life of it's own within me. I don't know what to do with it, it serves no purpose here. Were I to trip upon you there would be no way. Still, no way. My life changes with each child I bring forth to this world, and each is more beautiful and often more wondrous than the last. The aches I feel for each of you would kill each other, and me in the process. I am a mother, and their experience is more important than my own. I know this as surely as I know anything in this world. I try to live up to that. There is no space for you here, yet, here you are, in these words, in the longing that years after it all, years, I can finally express a thought. Buried beneath a husband and children and all the love that they all bring into my life. Happily buried. With this ache.

No sense.

It has no purpose here.

Yet here it is. Thank you for that, for intelligently and beautifully sweeping me off my chaotically crafted ass, never letting me forget that it is right now, this very second, which matters, so fill it. I have filled my seconds with beauty and love and growth and finally, a bit more growth, and I know that this warmth I feel wrapped around my shoulders is you, somewhere, feeling me as I feel you, deeply, inside, deep inside where the real me lives, the me that need not worry about responsibility and can and will run away with you to the ends of the earth. Thank you for taking me with you.

Gregory E. Burchett

"MO" (December 5, 2008)

T-Minus 80 days until Garrison's Murder.

I seem to have an MO when it comes time to rid myself of one man and move on to the next. It's the third time the same interests have occurred to me, so there is, at this point, no real way to avoid seeing the reality of my segue way behaviors.

First of all, I make sure that anything on My Wish List is purchased for me, but not by me. Really, it depends on how much money the man I am with makes, or how much money I am making, if worse comes to worse and I have to use my own cash. The last time, it was a whole lotta work clothes and anything from the house that I wanted, which included the only TV in the house. Uh, hey, I'd bought it. Sure, it was on credit and I declared bankruptcy, but ownership is ownership.

This time it was Brighton Collectibles and a new car.

Second of all, I start to look at my hands more and wonder if they wouldn't look better with a silk wrap, or perhaps bite the bullet and go fully into acrylics? This decision takes up quite a lot of time, I actually spend a good month considering it, and THEN, to top it off, I make sure that it is HIS decision. And that he pays for it. It just seems to work. The same fella who ultimately lost his ability to watch TV, for at least one evening, used to spend quite a lot of time drinking lattes while I got my nails done. That he paid for.

I don't like having my nails done. I can't get the same sensory sensations; it feels like my nails are wearing condoms, I suppose. For instance, when I pick my nose, I am not sure if the pick was fruitful or not until I can visually inspect what is under my nail.

Certainly I can no longer FEEL what might be under my nail given the condoms they are wearing.

My back also goes out. Lower back. Out.

Wiping down the counters, I seem to get my best work done. I smoke a little dope, and think a few thoughts. It's good for the soul. Much like a commercial mopping enterprise. Laying down and picking up water, the mop gliding back and forth, back and forth, swishing and gliding, effortless, simply bylaying down upon it the mop.

I am codependent. Or something.

I know what the behaviors of others are, and I look for those to fulfill my own needs. Like, Greg stopping what he is doing to take care of my needs, instead of me scheduling my needs at a more convenient time. I thought it was convenient, but it turns out that it wasn't that convenient, what with me having a full bladder and all. I did a dry run, so to speak, the day before, where I flipped the fuck out and learned a valuable lesson. Not that valuable, apparently, as the very next day I forgot and had to relearn it, at my own expense. I feel like I have achieved momentary states of utopia, heaven on earth, etc., without any indication that it was the manic side of whatever level of bipolarity I suffer from. Because it was simple peace.

Try, try, try again.

"MY NEW BOOK" (February 12, 2009)

T-Minus 11 days (264 hours) until Garrison's Murder.

The child awoke. She had been lost in something golden, much like the light streaming into her room. She waited there in the silence of the space and slowly sounds made their way into her awareness. Her ego recognized the causes and so began the days chatter, but always traveling with her, the space, and the silence of the space, the flow.

Had the preacher man told her, "It is through your every breath that you connect with the flow of the universe. Allow your mind to hear only your breath and you will discover God", he may have had a convert to small town religion. Not small town like 'small town' means anything, but that I lived in a small town, and it was a church located there, religious, I presume.

I'd asked him how he KNOWS there's a God.

And he said that I just had to have faith.

Like that was an answer.

Or maybe like faith was something available only to upper class citizens, because it was totally not coming to me like a lightbulb coming on that my question had been answered. Faith. Yes. Faith. Later in life I read that the brains of those with faith are different structurally than those without, upon autopsy. I am not sure if they'd asked the folks formerly residing in the brains, but I assume they would have had to.

Maybe they were 'the chosen' of whichever flavor of religion has those and you declare yourself to be a part of.

Chosen citizens with moms and dads at home, where the dad goes to work and the mom wears makeup and bras. Not citizens like me, their dad's in jail, their mom's braless as always in Texas maybe, living with the grandparents, in a new elementary school, after the one in Kaleva and that day where our lives changed forever for the first, or second, or third, or maybe fifth time, at the single wide trailer in the country. That day we waited a long, long time for our mom to get home and finally our grandpa came out all the way from Copemish and got us and told us to get our things, all the things we would need, that we were going to go home with him and be there with him and Grandma for awhile. We were 5 and 4, just. I don't know what we got, but I imagine it was not what we needed.

I asked that preacher man, but HOW do you have faith?

He patted me on the top of the head and stopped seeing me, and looked up at an approaching adult. I was dismissed. Perhaps it was my attire? I was poor, with no mom to dress me, and I was little. I'm sure my hair wasn't brushed well enough, it was very thick and wavy dark brown, always in my eyes and over my face. Life hadn't been easy to that point, and religion was heralded as, well, a religious experience. And that kind of experience seems to be what we are all after and all get the tingles from. I was looking for that. I'd heard the Lord's Prayer and talked to the kids at school or at the playground and I knew all about the Devil and going to hell. God was very important to people. But I didn't believe anything I heard; none of that rang true. But it was what we had, so I went to church for a religious experience. I didn't have one.

And religion and God were started in their paths toward dismissal. In spite of my grandma's jehovah's witnesses stuff, beautifully illustrated, peacefully and yet horrifyingly depicted stories of compliance with a God mandate or a visit of some bad stuff. Wowser. I was glad I was only a kid and didn't need to worry about that kind of stuff. I did a little forecasting and didn't see me worrying about it in the future, either, and that made me worry that I was a bad one, that the Devil must already have control of me. I paused and did a self survey.

Finding no Devil there either, I went further down that path of dispatching with religion.

That preacher man wasn't the only preacher man I questioned. I knew that you could get a bad seed in any profession – maybe he was new? There were none better than the first.

Yet, I talked to God. I was compelled to after I discovered that life was finite and I was going to one day die. That my grandfather was going to one day die was as terrifying.

I could feel an upward spiral of fear and suddenly, I was no longer a child of God, unconcerned with my physical body's ultimate destination and living purely and lovingly in the present, I was now just something that would be dead, just as many other things I had seen were dead. The idea of simply no longer existing like these things also seemed to no longer exist was a horrifying thought; would I too, be reduced to a smear of flesh and hair? Inconceivable. Yet true, it would seem.

He once stopped the rains long enough for me to get to my friend Jessica's house. She lives three miles out of town, on a beautiful stretch of road that I feel has special vibrations. The natural beauty of practically any square foot of earthen space in the northern part of Michigan is ripe with life, deep within that square foot of earth are essence and scent and nature and home and we are with it as it is with us.

You must ask God for forgiveness, you must ask God to ease your pain. Not with your words, but with your true essence. It is when you truly ask, when you truly have the capacity to receive, that God will ease your pain, and in the space where the pain was, and in the space throughout, God will fill this space with the certainty and love of the existence of pre love. Pure caring love. Pure, absolutely caring. Total care. It is when your trust is not in God (they say), or when your ego is so active that your essence cannot hear, so filled is it with the chatter of your ego. Trust in God is not an action that the ego can take. You cannot say to another that you trust in God. The utterance of these words does not impart this message. The utterance, the façade of these words does not open your heart. Trust in God, to me, a non religious person, are words. I've been told to Trust in God my entire life.

I pledge allegiance

To the flag

Of the United States of America

And to this republic

For which it stands

One nation

Under god

Indivisible

With liberty and justice for all

If your heart has no capacity to receive this love, it will not. You will suffer until your heart knows true sufferance, true pain. Your painful childhood? Your sexual abuse? Your exposure to violence and anger? Your neglect? Your neglect of others? Your exposure of others to violence and anger? Your infliction of sexual abuse upon another? Your infliction of painful memories upon your children? All of these, methods by which the human organism runs up against pain. You must know pain to know its counterpart. Bliss. Better than any ... (fill in the blank with whatever you currently enjoy a great deal of). The description must first include a feeling of ease. Ease about everything. Not a forced ease. Your ego is quiet. Your ego is not forcing anything. Your ego is asleep. You, the real you, the higher you, has merged with your lower self, and your lower self recognizes a superior being when it sees one. It is quiet, in respect and gratitude for being let in on The Secret, that the ego serves only as an actor in this grand play, the great folly, this life. Your lower self was relieved of its great anguish, its great pain, and shown its exact opposite. If there is a relationship between the experience of bliss and anguish, I feel grateful for the many experiences of anguish that my ego has observed, understanding that the anguish I experienced was caused directly by heeding my ego's advice. so that I may now know the peace I know.

It is a total absence of pain. To be relieved of the ego's demands of entertainment, pain, vilification. To feel in its place and throughout every other as yet unnoticed place within you, lay the knowledge of the very universe, to know without doubt that there is no more AND no less than us, the very best of us, the source from which we came and to which we will return, again, and again, and again. At the end I think there's a big party with a keg and everything. I'm off wheat right now so I'll bring a bottle of red; I have 80 bottles, at the moment. For medicinal use only.

There is so much more of the very best of what we are and absolutely none of the worst. The ego does not exist within us. There is so much more that there could never be emptiness. The ego's feelings of emptiness are a veil between your true essence, your higher self, and the flow, the source, love, God. The pain you accumulate builds so that you may know its converse, so that you may know God. Once you know God, once you are truly able to ask, from your very essence, for God to relieve you of your pain, you are already relieved of your pain. Because your lower self, your ego, has merged with your higher self, your true self, the flow, the source, love, God.

I'm writing this sentence, or the one above it, or one below it. I don't know. My son Gregory would like more crinkle puffs. I don't take much attention away from what I am doing, believing that I am in the flow while I am writing the truth as I know it (the only time I have ever been able to write). I glance around the kitchen counters; I don't see them. Hm. I go back to writing. I have to pee, I've had to pee for awhile, now that I notice it again. Crinkle puffs, mom? Shit. He needs to eat before his nap (his lunch is in the bag I can't find, terrible, I know, but not, and I'll tell you later why). Fine, I'm done. Look around some more, I'm back into some manic thinking, chasing one thought after another through the house and back and then back again and again. Those goddamn crinkle puffs could be anywhere, in any of the rooms. I'm redecorating my house while my soul takes on new adornment, another interesting facet of this experience, whatever this experience is. I am capable of creating beauty around me. One room, another, another, pick up a few things, thinking if I would just 'get with the flow' (literally) I would literally trip over those crinkle puffs. I've proven it to myself over and over again, or rather, the universe has. Ok, fine, go with the flow. Since nature was calling, I headed for the bathroom.

And wouldn't you know it, those goddamn crinkle puffs were on the counter.

Nature called. I listened.

When nature calls, you must listen. The universe is gifting you, and you must honor her gift with your inner silence.

Gregory E. Burchett

"MORE FINAL" (February 19, 2009)

T-Minus 3 days (72 hours) until Garrison's Murder

Spinning like a top

A child, arms wide, spinning, the faster you go, the faster the input and the greater the output

Hide and Seek, I Am

The age old game between children the ecstasy of hiding the thrill of searching

my heightened awareness

listening for a tell tale sound

vibrantly attuned to any vibrations

the hairs on the back of my neck are up, aware

scents travel by on the wind, stopping only briefly to connect

the tease of a towel still on the line, fluttering in the breeze

falsely alarm my senses

My blood pounds strong and steady, I am flowing with energy

There!

Is it! Yes! It is!

I run to investigate, fully engaged in finding that which would elude me

Missing The Links

But no.

Nothing here, at least not now.

I am still, pausing, attuned, attenuated, poised, here, tense, in this moment.

I am The Seeker.

And me, here, or maybe over there, if he gets closer!

there, maybe, even?

He's close, oh wow!

Oh, shit!

Run!!!

Hiding again, whew!

The heartbeat of a terrified rabbit, drumming within your chest

And the utter ecstacy and release of feeling safe after they'd been so fucking

close! Jesus CHRIST that was close!!!

Ecstacy.

Release.

That is all that exists. The joy of hiding, and the joy of seeking. The pain and release of being found, and then it is your turn to be at the opposing end of the spectrum, you are now the seeker.

Good customer service is service that can respond to the moment of the request. Period. You can only offer that if you are paying attention. I like attention.

Gregory and Garrison, having a wonderful time

Wonderful

Gales of Laughter upon gales of laughter

Then someone, or two someones, got lost in thought instead of being lost in the moment

And in the moment of inattention

Two worlds collided

And the laughter was dissolved into tears

Two bonked skulls

The baby was over it far before Gregory; his ego was far too invested after he'd received continued attention from his momma

I don't blame him. Anyone would.

Gregory continued to cry a bit more

He threw his head back, throwing himself into it, throwing his ego into it

I said stop your fucking BULLshit and get your ass into bed, my ego as far from this interaction as could be.

But I don't want to, he said, as far from tears as could be.

Missing The Links

Had I said, "Oh honey, please get up into bed and in just a minutes your head is going to stop hurting, I promise!"

His cries would still be going on as I write this

But they are not

No, in fact, he is 100% content, playing by himself in a process of discovery with the buttons on his daddy's bass amplifier currently sitting in the corner of our bedroom. Nature's call was heeded and the energy was released back into the universe. We all breathed easy.

Horrible mother?

To say 'fucking bullshit' to 3.5 year old?

Ego: Words are words, grow up, you fucking ninny.

God: If you are uncomfortable with all of the words in the language, it's because you are still a young soul, and young souls do not yet have mastery of their ego.

Like the person who wrote the sentence just above.

Birth Control

The Catholic Church has something going on with this, I think. Somebody down that line had a connection to God. I'm not sure if every religion has a policy for birth control. Folks who attended the Catholic Church, who ALSO had a relationship with God, practiced the Rhythm Method because their church told them to. I hear that the Rhythm Method doesn't work very well, like, about 60% of folks don't get knocked up. I'll check later. Anyway, so the point is, as God's chosen children, you will follow his guidance, because nature apparently wants you to have babies, right?? At least 40% of the time. Folks that do not have this relationship with God were not told by God to follow that method; for them, he has dispensed birth control in any number of forms which appeal to your particular personality.

Poor, crazy people: No birth control.

Regular joes: Lots of birth control.

Not so regular joes: Voracious breeders (the Kennedy's), live fast, and die young.

Homosexuality, Men

Homosexuality, Women

Heterosexuals,

Female Orgasm and Difficulty in Orgasm: It's difficult to orgasm for a lot of women. Most women. Not all.

Women simply have more difficulty maintaining steadiness; by nature, they fall prey to the rapid cycling that accompanies the birthing responsibilities. It's in their nature. Finding that balance requires a discipline that is difficult to maintain; you do the work, you get the rewards. We don't do the work.

Ego: Bullshit. I fucked his brains out.

God: Yes, but you should have been concentrating on fucking your OWN brains out.

Men, on the other hand, seem to just get the rewards. Most men. Not all.

They are far more able to maintain the steadiness of mind required to walk the tight-rope which is human orgasm, and they deserve it. They are men. They've earned it, lifetimes ago, and probably again now, in this lifetime. They make better leaders. If they are gay, or effeminate, not so. Too much feminine, not enough masculine. Too much ego, not enough God. A woman could not ascend to the throne, so to speak, but she is the plaything of God and as such, his. A woman's place is to serve man. Men shouldn't get too excited about this. A woman's place is to serve a man, not any man, but the real deal – at its height, the father figure. Ladies, don't feel bad about it. It is your nature.

A woman's heaven is to be tended to,

Her hell is to be denied

A man's heaven is to be entertained.

A man's hell is to be denied entertainment.

There is a delicate balance between the two needs. A female needs to be tended to and a male needs to be entertained. A relationship where the tending of one and the entertainment needs of the other are not met are troubled. This is true between the male and a female genders, regardless of which sexual apparatus they've come with.

Mother Earth has not properly tended to him and so Father Time denies her his attention. She's out of time, and it is the end of days. It's quite simple, isn't it?

As the universe expands, the female is on the rise. The universe is expanding. They know this, they just don't know why. It's probably getting faster, too, as it nears the curve to turn around the other way. When black women again rule the earth is when it will turn back around and go the other way, back to the ways of the barbarians. This is the end of times that religions refer to. They are right.

Goddamn you, Oprah. You, George W, and Barack Obama. You started it. You got us to love black women, Barack got us to embrace the idea of black and in charge, and George W. made certain that white guys have forever lost favor.

And the meek shall inherit the earth. This means that you, who did not pay attention to all that was happening around you, God's creation for his woman, being too meek, shall inherit it. All the rest of us, though, we're apparently getting reabsorbed into the love that is God. We are going home. How did we manage this? We connected to our breath. To our prana, in yogic circles, to our life source, our energy, to our Father.

You woman, you and your ego, you get to remain here on earth. And the end of days looks like it may be a reality after all.

Gay men are not forsaken. Only the gay men who did not get AIDS are forsaken. The others are in their glory, literally. Gay men are getting some help in the form of AIDS. God is bringing them into him.

He tells you what to do through your breath. Note your breath now. Stomach or chest? If it was your stomach, congratulations, you were mindful and listening with your heart. If it was your stomach, you were caught up in your own ego and are not sufficiently mindful. Pay more attention. It isn't called Paying Attention because it's free. You get what you pay for.

This is the way it is. Check some history books if you want to kind of gauge it. I have not (at this moment) referred to anything, and yet I think of Genghis Khan and the male having been at its all time high. How long ago was that? What else has happened in history and how can we gauge the male falling and the female rising?

Ego is the female. Ego is at an all time high. The entire universe does reek of it, doesn't it? Reality TV? Jesus Katie Christ, which of you fucking idiots watch that shit? Oh, nevermind, you, the meek. Yep, seriously. You're fucked, looks like. I'd switch to Discovery Channel.

A man's heaven is having his queen. His hell is to be pushed away from his plaything; his universe, his woman. He gets his toys taken from him, one at a time. This is his hell.

Female Managers: I am a strong woman. No one has ever, in their lives and lived to tell, told me what to do. Ok, not really like that, but sort of. I will not be moved. I will weigh each and every fact and if the facts are not at hand, then we are not making a decision. Others enjoy working with me, I am one of those who doesn't have anyone work 'for' me. But I am also one of those who does not work 'for' anyone, either. My military experience and the troubles (minor) that I found there while coming to terms to this component of my personality are telling; I find within me that which is reasonable, and I do not sway with the times. This means that I adhere to what I feel are the laws of nature. If that conflicts with societal law, that's the way it is.

Speeding and why I keep getting away with it: God has provided me with cop-free lanes of pleasure after pleasure. And he warned me of cops up ahead by instilling in me a sense of anxiety in order to slow down. It was only after I got really full of myself in 2001 that I got three tickets, in succession. I was 31 and I'd sped from one place to another only in between the times when

I get into the car, and then get out of the car, so, often enough. My point is; I was tuned in to the flow, as I am tuned into the flow right this minute. This doesn't make this sentence the best sentence that will ever be typed by my fingers, but it does make it the right one. How do I know? Because I am breathing with my stomach, and I am comfortable doing so. If you are breathing with your stomach right now, and comfortable doing so, then your decision in reading is the right one. If you are still reading, and your breath primarily with your chest, and you feel uncomfortable, then reading this is the wrong decision and you need to put it down. This does not mean that you won't pick it up again; you may. It could take you 50 years to read it. Doesn't matter. You will arrive where you will arrive when you are meant to arrive there. Might as well get comfy for the ride, you know? Snuggle right in to yourself; get really comfy; you're going to be with yourself every moment of every day. Stop. Listen. Pay attention. Truly see. Truly hear. Look to the location of the sound, pay attention. Focus. Breath.

It is here that you find God.

Garrison Lee Burchett, murdered February 23, 2009.

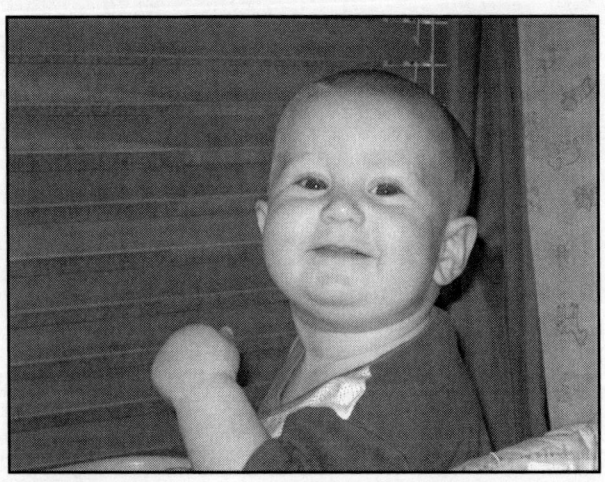

Chapter 6:
Living versus Breathing

As I sit here, trying to collect my thoughts on this last final chapter, I am finding it most difficult to describe what my future holds. I am having a hard enough time living in my present. I think the previous chapters were somewhat easier for me to write, because I concentrated on what happened, how I tried to deal with them, and my thoughts or feelings why they happened.

Hopefully, these words have been helpful to others…

This is more difficult – perhaps this part of my journey has just begun.

It is over four years since I found Garrison lying on the bed. It is over four years since I felt my life was destroyed, in so many ways. It has been over four years of fighting and battling, almost every day of my life, to rebuild what was torn apart.

It is over four years of my attempting to understand the totality of my experience.

I have struggled emotionally, I have struggled intellectually, I have struggled financially, and I have struggled professionally. To say that this experience has changed my life drastically would be an understatement.

I feel that I have "stabilized" my ship on the ocean. I may be adrift just a bit, but I am floating, and I am strong. I have a compass bearing on my "true north" which is Gregory's well-being. But in doing so, I couldn't be a good father if I also didn't enjoy my life for myself. Often people bury themselves in someone else's happiness (or misery), and in doing so, lose who they are. I don't want that for me.

If my taking care of Gregory is the only thing that mattered in my life, I wouldn't be taking care of Gregory very well, now would I?

I can't take care of Gregory, unless I take care of myself first.

I am doing that. There is so much more I could include in this book, which may give a broader perspective of my life. Some of this I unintentionally left out, and much of this I chose specifically not to include, for many reasons.

But I think the value of what I have done here isn't necessarily in where in my life I am now, and where my life may be headed.

Missing The Links

I have been told "don't leave them hanging, Greg! They want to know more!" I am smiling as I write this.

I appreciate that...

But I feel that the value of this book is in how someone can deal with a tragic event in their life, and put the shattered pieces back together again. The value of this book is in the recognition of my mistakes and observations, and perhaps someone can see similar circumstances in their lives. Perhaps this could help prevent another tragedy.

Isn't that really what this is all about?

I tried to think about what I should say. What kind of message, in its totality, am I attempting to offer any reader.

Is life a struggle? Yes.

Does life hurt? Yes.

Are there things that happen, for no apparent reason? Absolutely.

Does life go on? Unfortunately, yes; and fortunately, yes.

Because life does go on, having to wake up every day, and having someone really need you is all that I needed to live. Gregory indeed saved my life. Had he been home, and had Lori done what she intended with him as well – well, you know the rest.

This story I have shared began with a downward spiral, a focused effort to live day to day, to my attempt not to place too much blame on myself.

I sincerely hope that these words are read in their entire context, and not dissected piece, by miserable piece.

This is a story of tragedy, of blame, and of confusion. But, this is my story from my optimistic perspective.

I sincerely hope that these words I have shared will help at least one person recognize in a loved one (or in themselves) that something may be wrong, and that it is ok to ask for help. Perhaps, just perhaps, these words will save a life. Becoming involved with the Inland Empire Perinatal Mental Health Collaborative has given me a chance to convey this important message by making public appearances, and in actuality has given me the strength to write this book by sharing my experiences and pain with others.

I know that there are those who have already been helped by my tragedy, tremendously.

If this book can help that happen again, then just perhaps, it was all worth it.

So I decided to keep this chapter short and sweet.

Life is good…

I play sports with Gregory. I help coach his baseball and football teams. I love to live life through his eyes. Watching him in school, watching him surrounded by friends, and watching him smile and hearing his laughter is everything to me. He is excelling in school academically and socially, and I couldn't be any more proud of him than I am.

Life is good…

I have rekindled and fostered relationships with loved ones and family. Slowly, but surely, I am focusing on relationships that I had let slip away just a bit. I still have a lot of work to do here. True love for friendships are too valuable to not fight for.

Life is good…

I have a good heart, and optimistic outlook, and I feel as if I am still a big kid.

Life is good…

I have begun having more fun.

Life is good…

Heck. I wrote a book.

Epilogue

Dr. Marjorie Rust, Ed. D.
Educational Psychologist

Love is an enigma. Why is it seemingly so easy for some people to feel this powerful emotion and follow it into a fulfilling life while others look for it and never find it? Never find it to have a "right fit", so they keep running from one "lover" to another leaving wreckage behind.

This is Lori. An attractive, bright, self reliant young woman whose only true loves are her children, one of whom she murders, while her fifteen year old son Nick, whom she adores, is sitting just outside the room. She was a strict mother, so whatever Nick was told to do that day, he did. He sat, and waited, and wondered.

I first met Lori when she was a graduate student of mine. After she graduated we stayed in touch and became friends. Over the years I learned about her life growing up. Various men her mother brought home and how afraid Lori and her brother would be, hiding under the bed. Their "moving" in the middle of the night, because the rent was due the next day. Sometimes for the third or fourth month in a row.

She seemed to have survived pretty well, except for the men she brought into her life. Not the men per se, but her relationships with them. Lori is the closest to a nymphomaniac I have ever known. One example of her sometimes confused values: I said, you could have become a rich prostitute and she said, "oh no it would not be right to take money for the pleasure."

All of the men I met were pretty nice guys and worshiped the ground she walked on, especially Greg. He was so in love with her that he suffered her moodiness and sometime anger believing that a stable married life would "make her better." It did not.

When I was teaching I used a book, *Love is not Enough*, *(Bettleheim, Bruno, 1950)* regarding emotionally disturbed children. The title says it all about any relationship - child to child, child to parent, parent to child, adult to adult. No one can cure another person be it physical or emotional. All any of us can do is try to guide them to "help themselves" get better. This is true of physical health decisions as well as mental health problems. That is what any good doctor or mental health professional does.

Consequently when we love someone we can only try to get them to get help. Lori does not know what stable love and home life entails. She tried three times and became a fantastic mother, but never a wife. With her children she seems to be able to give of herself and believe that the love will be returned. Friends, colleagues and her three husbands would tell anyone, she could have been mother of the year.

Thus, when she told Nick to stay there and she would be out in a minute, at fifteen, that was exactly what he did. Even when it was found that his worst fears were true, she had killed his baby brother, he appealed to people to not hurt his mother. There was nothing he could have done, about what was going on the other side of that door, but he will never forget. He greatly needs therapy to work things through for himself.

Gregory misses his baby brother more than he does his mother. Despite the years separating Gregory and Garrison, they had been raised to be close. With all of Greg's problems and struggles since the murder of Garrison the one thing he has devoted his life to is raising Gregory to be a normal, well adjusted, loving little boy. Someday he may want to meet his mother again, that will have to be his choice, not hers.

Lori's daughter (from her first marriage) has probably come through all of the chaos and trauma the best. Cass, is very much like her mother except for one quality Lori never found, how to love another person. That is Cass's legacy, it seems she may understand that to love someone means to share not just her body, but herself with that special person.

The young woman I have known all of these years will do well in prison. Lori always appeared to tolerate authority, so I am sure she is a model prisoner. Her intelligence and her ability to manipulate others will carry her a long way in surviving. She is great at teaching computer skills. She is well organized and relates to her students.

The one thing she will not be able to do is run away from any problems that arise. This has been the pattern all her life. Now, she will have to stand up and face things until she realizes there is no going back. Lori did not kill Garrison in anger, she says that she does not know why she did it. Greg's love blinded him to her needs and he thought he could "save her" - he could not.

As in any tragedy, the number of victims in this event are many more than the actual "players". Garrison is gone, but those left to suffer his death will never be free.

CPSIA information can be obtained at www.ICGtesting.com
Printed in the USA
LVOW13s2013270913

354320LV00003B/212/P